Protecting Personally Identifiable Information:

A Guide for College and University Administrators

Peter F. McLaughlin

© 2011 Council on Law in Higher Education
All Rights Reserved
Published in the United States of America

Disclaimer: The information contained herein is designed to provide information and analysis to assist people involved and interested in higher education law and policy. IT IS NOT A SUBSTITUTE FOR PROFESSIONAL LEGAL ADVICE. The views expressed are those of the authors alone and do not necessarily reflect the views of CLHE.

ISBN: 978-0-6154494-9-4

Library of Congress Control Number: 2011922943

ABOUT CLHE

The Council on Law in Higher Education (CLHE) is a national nonprofit organization providing independent and easy-to-understand analysis of timely policy and legal issues for administrators and attorneys.

Since 1998, hundreds of institutions from across the country have turned to CLHE for its extensive tracking of major developments, and more importantly, the organization's insightful analysis and perspective on how these developments will impact their campuses.

Members receive a regular publication tracking major developments, special law and policy reports, free teleseminars, major discounts on webinars and books, plus much more.

CLHE membership is extremely inexpensive, and unlike most organizations, there is no limit to how many people on a campus can receive the invaluable benefits.

Visit www.clhe.org to learn more about CLHE and how you can become a part of this important organization.

Council on Law in Higher Education
9386 Via Classico West
Wellington, Florida 33411
Phone: (561) 792-4440
Fax: (561) 792-4441
Web: www.clhe.org

ABOUT THE LEAD AUTHOR

Peter F. McLaughlin is senior counsel with Foley & Lardner LLP and a member of the firm's Privacy, Security & Information Management Practice. His experience as a corporate lawyer and business advisor includes international privacy, information security, information technology (IT) compliance, and IT transactions. Prior to joining Foley, Mr. McLaughlin was in-house counsel for over eight years for different U.S. companies. This included assistant general counsel and the first global privacy leader for Cardinal Health, Inc., a Fortune 20 company with operations in over 30 countries. He was responsible for driving the strategy, policy and implementation of the company's first global privacy program. Mr. McLaughlin is also former assistant general counsel for Sun Microsystems.

ABOUT THE CONTRIBUTING AUTHORS

Kenny W. Hoeschen is an associate with Foley & Lardner LLP and is a member of the Information Technology & Outsourcing and Privacy, Security & Information Management Practices. Prior to joining the firm, Mr. Hoeschen was a senior consultant with Greenbrier & Russel, where he defined and developed strategic IT plans for both government and private entities.
(Contribution: Chapter 1)

Chanley T. Howell is a partner in the Intellectual Property Department of Foley & Lardner LLP, and he is a member of the firm's Privacy, Security & Information Management Practice. Mr. Howell represents companies in a variety of technology law areas, such as compliance with data privacy and security requirements; FTC privacy requirements; state data privacy, security and breach notification laws; regulatory risk assessment and compliance audits; privacy and information security policies; records retention, destruction and management policies, online privacy policies, social media policies.
(Contribution: Chapter 4)

Matthew A. Karlyn is a partner with Foley & Lardner LLP and is a member of the firm's Information Technology & Outsourcing Practice. Mr. Karlyn is also a member of the firm's Privacy, Security & Information Management Practice. Mr. Karlyn has extensive experience in privacy, security and information management matters and routinely advises clients on state, federal and international restrictions on the use of information; compliance with state security breach notification laws; and drafting and implementing privacy and security policies. Mr. Karlyn has extensive experience with transactions relating to outsourcing and information technology, including IT outsourcing, technology licensing, business process outsourcing, systems integration, cloud computing and software development.
(Contribution: Chapter 1)

Meaghan McCluskey is a Senior Privacy Research Lawyer with Nymity Inc. and a Certified Information Privacy Professional. She began working for Nymity in 2008, after articling for the Information and Privacy Commissioner of Ontario.
(Contribution: Chapter 5)

Eileen R. Ridley is a partner with Foley & Lardner LLP. She is managing partner of the firm's San Francisco office and vice chair of the Litigation Department. Ms. Ridley is a member of the Privacy, Security & Information Management Practice. Ms. Ridley is a co-chair of Foley's Privacy Litigation Task Force and the former co-chair of the Litigation Department training program. Ms. Ridley has extensive experience in litigating, arbitrating and trying complex commercial matters for a variety of industries including the high-tech, oil and gas, telecommunications, construction, insurance and health care industries, covering ERISA litigation, commercial disputes, and employment issues.
(Contribution: Chapter 2)

William T. Yoon is a former associate with Foley & Lardner LLP and is currently privacy counsel with Google, Inc. Mr. Yoon practices in the area of privacy and business litigation and is a graduate of Northwestern University Law School.
(Contribution: Chapter 7)

ABOUT THE EDITORS

Daren Bakst is the President of the Council on Law in Higher Education, which he founded in 1998. In this position, he has written and presented extensively on privacy and information security issues. He was the author of CLHE's 1999 book <u>Student Privacy on Campus</u> and co-editor of CLHE's 2004 book <u>Privacy in the 21st Century</u>. Mr. Bakst is widely cited and published, including in publications such as *USA Today*, *The Wall Street Journal*, the *Chronicle of Higher Education*, the *Washington Times*, *Student Aid Transcript*, and *AOL News*.

He has worked for numerous public policy organizations on both the federal and state level, focusing on a wide range of legal and regulatory issues. He served as Policy Counsel for the National Legal Center for the Public Interest, which recently merged into one of the most prominent national think tanks, the American Enterprise Institute. He currently serves as Director of Legal and Regulatory Studies for the John Locke Foundation, a North Carolina based think tank, where he focuses on a wide range of issues, including privacy issues. Mr. Bakst received his M.B.A. from the George Washington University, his J.D. from the University of Miami, and his LL.M. in Law and Government from the American University.

Peter F. McLaughlin is senior counsel with Foley & Lardner LLP and a member of the firm's Privacy, Security & Information Management Practice. His experience as a corporate lawyer and business advisor includes international privacy, information security, information technology (IT) compliance, and IT transactions. Prior to joining Foley, Mr. McLaughlin was in-house counsel for over eight years for different U.S. companies. This included assistant general counsel and the first global privacy leader for Cardinal Health, Inc., a Fortune 20 company with operations in over 30 countries. He was responsible for driving the strategy, policy and implementation of the company's first global privacy program. Mr. McLaughlin is also former assistant general counsel for Sun Microsystems.

VI

TABLE OF CONTENTS

PREFACE   **1**

PART I
The Risks of Maintaining Personally Identifiable Information

   CHAPTER 1   **7**
   Data Breaches on Campus

   CHAPTER 2   **25**
   Recent Trends in Data Security Litigation and Regulatory
   Enforcement

PART II
What Federal and State Laws Apply to Securing Data?

   CHAPTER 3   **37**
   The Gramm-Leach-Bliley Safeguards Rule

   CHAPTER 4   **47**
   State and Federal Laws on Social Security Numbers

   CHAPTER 5   **57**
   State Breach Notification Laws

PART III
Practical Steps to Protect Information and Respond to Breaches

   CHAPTER 6   **69**
   Protecting an Institution's Information

   CHAPTER 7   **87**
   Responding to an Incident

APPENDIX   **103**
State Prohibitions on the Use of Social Security Numbers,
Applicable to both Postsecondary Institutions and Other Entities

ENDNOTES   **115**

VIII

PREFACE

It is perhaps obvious to most people that information about us – personal information, health information, financial information, credit card details, and so forth – is increasingly electronic. Arguably, the vast majority of information is now created electronically. There are many possible ramifications of this. One impact is that it is easier to manipulate and analyze the information we have collected. Another is that it becomes easier to move and share vast amounts of data. Unfortunately, it also becomes easier to lose significant volumes of information, and for people to misuse the information.

Because this guide focuses on higher education, it makes sense that the emphasis be on the protection of personally identifiable information. Personally identifiable information is in many ways a fundamental currency within an institution. It is collected and evaluated upon application; it evolves through the individual's life at the institution, whether student or faculty; and it typically encompasses highly private, sensitive information that if lost, stolen, or misused, would harm someone. Because of this, personally identifiable information has become increasingly regulated as well.

The personally identifiable information commonly collected by colleges and universities, including information like students' and applicants' names, addresses, dates of birth, social security numbers, financial records, tax records, and medical records, are valuable to those who wish to profit by illegally accessing and distributing this information.[1]

Institutional staff and faculty also entrust significant personal information to an employer, as do patients at a college health clinic or university's academic medical center. College students themselves are also attractive targets to identity thieves and are estimated to comprise approximately one-third of all identity theft victims.[2] Students are often willing to share their personal information on social networking sites and, because they have fewer financial obligations, often have more disposable income than working people.[3] Their fresh credit histories also allow identity thieves to more easily gain access to new lines of credit.[4] Finally, because students are less likely to monitor their credit histories and more likely to change their mailing address frequently, early indications of identity theft may go unnoticed.[5]

None of those suggestions should come as a surprise to a reader of most daily newspapers. The news seems to contain weekly reports of data breaches, networks hacked, laptops lost, and (increasingly) criminals prosecuted for their roles. Colleges and universities present fertile ground for these unfortunate events because of their substantial information and a typically inconsistent means for protecting that data.

Privacy Rights Clearinghouse indicates that over the five and a half years from January 2005 through September 15, 2010, over 1,700 data breach incidents have involved over 500 million records across all sectors.[6] There are volumes of publicly available information that speak to the vulnerability of information held by higher education institutions. While the size of these incidents vary significantly, as do the causes, they range from a 93,000 record incident at Buena Vista University to 30,000 records from Penn State University and over 230,000 records stolen by a hacker from UNC Chapel Hill.[7]

In its 2010 Data Breach Investigations Report,[8] Verizon and the United States Secret Service determined that 70 percent of data breaches result from external agents and when insiders are involved 51 percent of breaches involve regular employees, as opposed to those in any special position of trust or responsibility. The challenge for any organization, then, is realizing that there are a great many people either intentionally or unintentionally releasing personal information. Furthermore, because so many of the affected schools have taken preventative steps to prepare for such an event, it should be clear that for any institution the question is not *if* but *when* a data breach will occur.

As we will see in the opening chapters of this guide, higher education institutions constitute a significant percentage of reported data breaches, and the risks of private litigation and regulatory enforcement are increasing. While private individuals have had difficultly pursuing legal claims for data breaches, regulators and attorneys general play an assertive consumer protection role. Concurrently and especially when credit card data is involved, card issuing banks and legislators are increasingly likely to hold financially responsible the organization that lost the credit card information.

The second part of this guide begins to explain the myriad federal and state laws governing use of personal information. One of the difficulties with United States data security laws is that information may be governed by different rules depending upon the context. For example, credit card data in a campus store is subject to one set of rules but when that credit card is used for a co-pay at a health center, another set of rules also applies. The Gramm-Leach-Bliley Act (GLB)[9] requires that colleges and universities apply security measures to safeguard certain personal financial information. The federal Red Flags Rules[10] require institutions to develop plans to mitigate the likelihood and potential impact of identity theft. In one context, a social security number (SSN) may be considered protected health information, regulated by the Health Insurance Portability and Accountability Act (HIPAA),[11] the federal health privacy law. In another context, state breach notification or social security protection laws may dictate obligations surrounding the SSN.

Finally, the third and last part of this guide provides practical tips on what is expected of institutions to protect personal information and how to handle data breaches. Having outlined the risks in part one, and the federal and state laws in part two, part three will review measures to reduce the risk and to increase the chances that when something happens it can be managed.

PREFACE

The unfortunate fact of life in our electronic world, however, is that these data breaches are unlikely to diminish until significantly better practices are adopted. This is not to say that the loss of old-fashioned paper with sensitive information does not happen without serious consequences, but that the potential for scale and impact is greater in our electronic age. Planning can help to manage these risks, though, and through protective steps and establishment of an emergency response plan, most institutions should be able to reduce the impact to them and their constituents from any security breach events.

In a sense, any organization that experiences a data loss suffers in multiple ways. There is initially the problem of redirecting resources to respond to the breach, determine its source, and address whatever weakness contributed to the event. The second level of cost to the organization is potential legal, financial and reputational harm. The cost outlays for notification letters, call centers, and consultants alone can be significant, apart from the possible need to reimburse third parties. Finally, enforcement continues to increase, both at the state level by attorneys general and the federal level by the Federal Trade Commission, the United States Department of Health & Human Services, and other agencies.

Evolving standards and methods to protect information benefit higher education while also presenting the difficulty of identifying, assessing, and applying these safeguards. The hackers who seek out the most valuable databases have time and resources, and should not be confused with bored teenagers without focus or discipline. Therefore, a school needs to monitor and continue to improve practices and recommendations to defend against bad actors, thoughtless employees as well as potential inquiries from regulators.

Like documentation for an individual's home insurance policy, much of this effort begins with an understanding of what information the college or university has, where it is, and what it is worth. While placing a value on student social security numbers or credit card files may not seem right, each has value, either to the organization, to the individual, or to a potential thief. Without knowing what information is within the system, it is extremely difficult to protect that information effectively.

The purpose of this guide is to assist college and university administrators, counsel, and staff to understand the particular risks higher education faces, the regulatory landscape, as well as steps to protect that data and comply with relevant rules. Because any post-incident review or criticism will come with the benefit of hindsight, the more that a school can appreciate its risk, the better it will be able to responsibly manage the institution's resources.

Peter F. McLaughlin
Boston, January 2011

PART I:

THE RISKS OF MAINTAINING PERSONALLY IDENTIFIABLE INFORMATION

CHAPTER ONE

DATA BREACHES ON CAMPUS

Sources of Data Breaches at Colleges and Universities

Colleges and universities have, in recent years, become a frequent source of breaches involving personal information and sensitive data. As illustrated in Figure 1, approximately 20 percent of all publicly reported data breaches originated from the education sector, with the vast majority of those coming from institutions of higher education.[12] Of those data breaches, the vast majority are a result of lost or stolen data, malicious attacks, or inadvertent disclosure of personally identifiable information over the Internet, as displayed in Figure 2.[13] Consideration of the causes of data breaches and the various methods and effectiveness of responses to them can provide guidance for how colleges and universities can address the risks associated with the storing of sensitive data and equip schools with the information needed to effectively respond in the event of a security breach.

> **IMPORTANT POINT**
>
> "approximately 20 percent of all publicly reported data breaches originated from the education sector, with the vast majority of those coming from institutions of higher education."

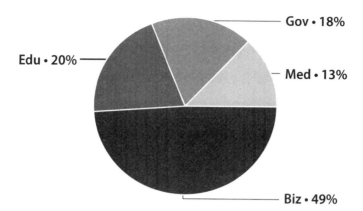

Figure 1. Data Breaches by Business Type. Source: Open Security Foundation / DataLossDB (www.datalossdb.org). Used by Permission. "Edu" is treated by DataLossDB as primarily higher education, although there are reports of primary and secondary school incidents within the database.

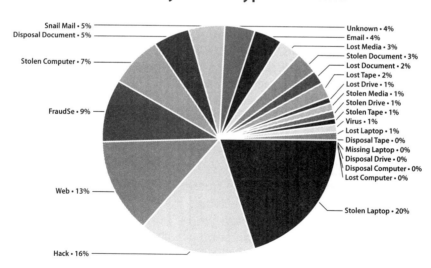

Figure 2. Data Breaches by Business Type. Source: Open Security Foundation / DataLossDB (**www.datalossdb.org**). Used by permission.

Institutional Computer Systems are Attractive Targets

College and university computer systems are often attractive targets for thieves because the networks are designed to allow access by faculty and students, the information contained on the college and university systems is considered to be particularly valuable, and college students themselves are considered to be attractive targets because of their financial situation.

College and university networks may represent a path of least resistance due to a frequent philosophy of making information more available and therefore employing less rigorous security measures. Compared with their corporate counterparts, academic networks are typically designed to be more open so as to better accommodate the diverse needs of the college's or university's faculty, staff, and student users.[14] Fred Cate, a law professor and director of the Center for Applied Cybersecurity Research at Indiana University, further believes that higher education is a juicy target because it compiles so much information in so many places.[15]

Decentralized Networks Add Risk

The tendency toward access and availability of information is compounded by the fact that individual academic departments are sometimes permitted to administer their own systems. For instance, following a 2006 data breach at the University of Delaware, Karl Hassler, the University's associate director for Information Technologies, stated, "There are many locally administered systems on campus that can from time to time become vulnerable to unauthorized access, including physical theft."[16]

The advantages of relatively open, available information systems and decentralized control must be judged against the importance of the information and the risk of loss. Colleges and

> **IMPORTANT POINT**
>
> "Decentralized security administration may hinder a college's or university's ability to ensure that security policies are being observed, that security patches are timely applied, that system access is limited to authorized users, and that intrusions are addressed properly."

universities must balance the need for libraries and other research facilities to have more open access to data with the need to keep sensitive information concentrated and secure.[17] Decentralized security administration may hinder a college's or university's ability to ensure that security policies are being observed, that security patches are timely applied, that system access is limited to authorized users, and that intrusions are addressed properly.[18] Budget constraints have also been blamed for preventing schools from keeping pace with investments in network security necessary to guard against new and sophisticated threats to their computer systems.[19]

Most Frequent Types of Data Breaches

As illustrated in Figure 2, an analysis of breaches at colleges and universities for the period of January 2000 through September 2010, collected from the Open Security Foundation's DataLossDB database, shows that the most common sources of data breaches were from laptops, storage media, and documents that were lost, stolen, or improperly discarded. These breach causes constituted approximately 34 percent of all breaches reported during that period. External threats from hacking and malicious intrusions constituted approximately 33 percent of all breaches reported during that period.[20]

Verizon Business Services published a report in the spring of 2010 in conjunction with the United States Secret Service titled the 2010 Data Breach Investigations Report.[21] While not specific to higher education, the report identified a number of data points and trends that apply to organizations with sensitive information.

Rarely A Single Cause

There is rarely a single, precise cause for a data incident. Verizon reports that 70 percent of data breaches resulted from external agents, indicating that hacking may continue to threaten databases. At the same time, 48 percent of reported breaches were caused by insiders, according to the Verizon report.[22] This may mean that insiders – university staff, administrators, faculty and potentially students – contribute to a significant amount of data loss.

Given the high percentage of external threats, the insider component could range from malign staffer to an individual who unwittingly downloaded malware. Because much of these data incidents continue to occur through computer systems, one of the important notes to all administrators is that the value of monitoring computer network traffic and log files "cannot be overstated. The signs are there; we just need to get better at recognizing them," says Verizon.[23]

Data Breaches through Lost, Stolen, or Discarded Data are Most Common Type of Breach at Institutions

At colleges and universities, data breaches as a result of lost, stolen, or discarded data[24] are slightly more common than breaches originating from malicious computer attacks such as an individual who intentionally gained unauthorized network access to an institution's computer system through "hacking."[25]

The widespread adoption of laptop computers and portable storage devices has made it easier than ever for vast amounts of sensitive data to be lost or stolen. Such devices are specifically designed to be lightweight and easily transported, making them easier to steal or to misplace inadvertently. Personally identifiable information is frequently stored on these devices without proper protection such as encryption. This means that the sensitive information is potentially vulnerable when anyone finding the device can plug the device into a laptop and see the data.

Accidental Disclosure of Data

Accidental disclosure of sensitive data trails malicious attacks and lost, stolen, or discarded data as the third largest source of data breaches in higher education.[26] As an example, in 2007, nearly 90,000 individuals

> **IMPORTANT POINT**
>
> "At colleges and universities, data breaches as a result of lost, stolen, or discarded data are slightly more common than breaches originating from malicious computer attacks such as an individual who intentionally gained unauthorized network access to an institution's computer system through 'hacking.'"

> **IMPORTANT POINT**
>
> "It is important that people entrusted with college or university laptop computers or other portable devices that contain personally identifiable information protect the physical security of those machines. However, ensuring that a portable storage device is physically secured does not alleviate the need to encrypt sensitive data stored on those devices."

affiliated with Stony Brook University had their names and social security numbers exposed when they were accidentally posted on the University's web site.[27] The University became aware of the incident after the database file that had accidently been published on a University web server was indexed by Google's search engine crawler.[28] Although Google had indexed the data only 24 hours prior, it is unclear how long the data had been available on the web server. The University notified affected individuals two weeks later and advised individuals to place fraud alerts on their credit files.[29]

Institutions Should Not Forget the Physical Security of Machines

It is important that people entrusted with college or university laptop computers or other portable devices that contain personally identifiable information protect the physical security of those machines. However, ensuring that a portable storage device is physically secured does not alleviate the need to encrypt sensitive data stored on those devices.

Proper security measures typically involve a *combination* of administrative policies and procedures, technology tools, and physical safeguards.

Physical Security

Case Study #1

When an external computer hard drive was stolen from Georgetown University in January, 2008, it was stolen from a locked University office.[30] It was later determined that the data on the drive included the unencrypted names and matching social security numbers of approximately 38,000 individuals.[31] As a result, the data could be copied simply by connecting the external drive to another computer.

After beginning a joint investigation with local law enforcement and the Secret Service, Georgetown began to notify all 38,000 individuals via email and standard mail, provided a toll-free hotline to affected individuals to receive information regarding the breach, recommended that affected individuals file fraud alerts with the credit rating agencies, and provided affected individuals with one year of a prepaid credit monitoring service at no charge to them.

Despite these measures, many students and alumni expressed frustration with the slow pace of investigation and notification.[32] One commentator in The Hoya, Georgetown's student newspaper where the breach was first reported, commented, "How appropriate is it that the student newspaper should be the one to tell all of these folks that their information could now be on the black market?"[33] Following the breach, Georgetown implemented additional measures to conduct a thorough inventory of the University's systems to identify where personally identifiable information is used, stored, accessed, and transferred.[34]

Case Study #2

A breach similar to the Georgetown University event occurred at Cornell University in June, 2009. In that instance, an employee was given access to a laptop computer containing sensitive information in order to complete file processing tasks. Contrary to University policy, the sensitive data on the laptop, consisting of names and social security numbers of more than 45,000 students and faculty, was not encrypted.[35]

After being left in a "physically unsecure environment," the computer was stolen and police were unable to recover it over the following weeks.[36] While the University stated that there was no evidence that the personal information had been exploited, the University nonetheless had to spend significant time and resources addressing the potential breach and complying with applicable state security breach and notice laws, including providing credit monitoring services and identity theft and restoration services to potentially affected individuals.[37]

Because portable devices such as laptop computers are an attractive target for theft and because it is nearly impossible to completely prevent portable devices from being lost or stolen, security solutions cannot rely on the diligence of users alone. However, the adoption of policies requiring the encryption of sensitive data is an incomplete solution.

Technology Can Support Policies

In the Georgetown and Cornell breaches, both universities had policies in place that required encryption of sensitive data and in both cases the data that was compromised had not been encrypted.[38] Alternative approaches that may have prevented those breaches include:

1. Adopting a policy prohibiting the local storage of sensitive data on portable devices altogether[39] or

2. Bypassing reliance on the user to follow encryption policies by implementing self-encrypting hard drives or software that automatically encrypts the entire contents of the laptop computer.[40]

Under the first solution, when the use of sensitive data is required, users may still access sensitive data but they do so through an encrypted session on a secured network server. The technology is configured so that the user is prevented from creating a copy of the sensitive data on a laptop computer or other portable storage device.[41] The second solution simply encrypts all data, rather than relying on the user to select which information should be secured. These solutions may reduce the chance that sensitive data will be exposed as a result of lost or stolen portable devices.[42]

Data Breaches through Malicious Attacks

A "malicious" attack, as the term implies, involves bad intent, as opposed to an incident that is the result of an accident or oversight. Malicious attacks do not arise solely from external forces, though, as insiders (employees, students, or officials) are equally capable of being driven by bad intentions.[43]

According to the data in Figure 2, approximately 33 percent of data breaches are the result of malicious computer attacks such as unlawful remote Internet access, unauthorized intranet access, and the ever-present threat of malware.[44] One example of a costly electronic attack occurred in November, 2006 when UCLA system administrators noticed a suspiciously large amount of activity on one of the University's database servers.[45] A preliminary investigation revealed that the server had been compromised and was under a sophisticated, well-coordinated attack.

Colleges and universities must also be on the lookout for malicious attacks that originate internally. Malicious attacks can arise from insiders who gain unauthorized access to certain files or who use their legitimate access to do unauthorized things (also referred to as "exceeding authorization"). These actions may take the form of emailing files to personal email accounts, copying information to USB drives, or posting information to the web. The motivations for such actions obviously vary significantly.

CHAPTER 1: DATA BREACHES ON CAMPUS

Internal Malicious Attacks

Case Study #1

A dissatisfied computer engineering student of the University of Delaware decided to take matters of University policy into his own hands.[46] The student monitored wireless Internet signals to capture his professor's network password and subsequently used the password to reschedule the date of an upcoming exam which some students had complained conflicted with another class.[47]

When the professor discovered he could no longer access his email account due to the changed password he promptly alerted campus police to the intrusion and the exam eventually proceeded on the originally scheduled date. The University caught the student after receiving an anonymous tip, but not before it had incurred more than $10,000 in expenses related to the investigation and repairs to the network. A data security breach such as this highlights the vulnerability of, and costs incurred by, institutions of higher education from even relatively minor intrusions.

Case Study #2

In another incident, two students at California State University Fullerton were each charged with conspiracy, wire fraud, identity theft, and unauthorized computer access for hacking into University computers and changing their grades.[48] One of the students had been employed by a University department and abused his position to gain access to unauthorized files. The University detected the record manipulation while performing a routine grade audit, and promptly turned the students' names over to the FBI Cyber Crime Task Force. The students faced academic sanctions including suspension, expulsion, and a loss of diploma along with up to five criminal indictments.

Meanwhile, the University was stuck with the expenses associated with repairing their systems and pursuing enforcement action against the perpetrators.[49]

The threat posed by an individual hacking into computer systems to gain unauthorized access varies based on his or her objectives, but any intrusion, regardless of intention, can result in severe costs to the victimized institution. While some digital attackers clearly intend harm, others' intentions are relatively benign.

> IMPORTANT POINT
>
> **"Colleges and universities face significant tangible and intangible costs resulting from data breaches. "**

Costs of Data Breaches to Institutions

Colleges and universities face significant tangible and intangible costs resulting from data breaches. For example, expenses for conducting a forensic investigation, notifying affected individuals, and possibly providing identity theft monitoring and other services to protect the affected individuals commonly range from the tens of thousands to several million dollars depending on the size of the breach and the number of individuals and records affected.[50] The institution will likely suffer intangible harm due to negative publicity and decreased goodwill in the community and among students and alumni.

Costs to Institutions Case Study

From March, 2005 until June, 2006, Ohio University suffered five distinct data breach events.[51] The longest lasting breach continued for over a year before it was discovered by the FBI.[52] Social security numbers, medical records, and other personal information of an estimated 173,000 students, employees, patients, and contractors were compromised in addition to detailed medical infor-

CHAPTER 1: DATA BREACHES ON CAMPUS

mation on about 60,000 individuals.[53] The University's costs for consulting, computer, and mailing costs necessary to address the breach were close to $1 million.[54]

Soon after, a lawsuit seeking class-action status was filed by two Ohio University alumni alleging a violation of their right to privacy.[55] The plaintiffs requested that Ohio University be ordered to pay for a court-administered credit monitoring service for all individuals whose personal identifiable information *may* have been exposed.[56] Financial compensation was also sought for those who suffered financial losses from identity theft caused by the data breaches.[57]

One high profile data security intrusion at Ohio University is now thought to have been caused by individuals who used the servers to store and distribute copies of bootlegged movies, but who did not in fact access sensitive data stored on the servers.[58] This event highlights how even an intrusion with relatively harmless intentions can have lasting repercussions for the victimized college or university. Events such as these spawn costs beyond merely responding to the intrusion. Compromised institutions experience loss of available resources and system performance due to the pirating of the system's utility and resources while the access remains undetected, financial losses in the form of spent wages and purchased prevention and response measures to circumvent intrusions, and, finally, ensuing liability in case any sensitive data *is* compromised. Two years after the intrusion, Ohio University was still dealing with its effects: two former Ohio University officials who were fired for failing to prevent the attack continued to press a suit against the University for allegedly trying to cover up details of the breach and for their wrongful terminations.[59]

Impact on Institutional Reputation

Damage to an institution's reputation, especially for colleges and universities that depend on donations from alumni, can also be a steep cost. News outlets carried several stories of outraged Ohio University alumni during that University's recent series of data breaches.[60] Many of the interviewed alumni expressed their intention to withhold donations from their alma mater as punishment for the events.[61] One alumna, who earned her degree in 1955 and whose personal data was contained in the exposed alumni-relations database felt so betrayed that she cancelled her plans to leave a significant endowment to the University in her will.[62] Such high profile events may also have the effect of discouraging new applicants from applying to or attending the college or university. While difficult to measure in terms of dollars, the public relations nightmare that commonly follows a data security breach can be significant. Furthermore, as highlighted in Chapter 2 on litigation and enforcement, individual plaintiffs have found it difficult to establish the financial harm that is typically required for a tort claim. However, in the context of credit card data losses, it is increasingly likely that an institution will have to reimburse a bank that has had to reissue credit cards to affected individuals.

Table of Potential Costs to Institutions

Direct Costs	Indirect Costs
Legal fees	Reputation generally
Consultant and forensic expenses	Internal resources redirected
Mailings and call center	Alumni relations
Credit monitoring services	

Costs to Affected Individuals

Even if exposed personally identifiable information is never exploited for criminal purposes, the time and money required of an affected individual to avoid identity theft can be enormous and especially onerous on students who are frequently on a more limited

> **IMPORTANT POINT**
>
> "Even if exposed personally identifiable information is never exploited for criminal purposes, the time and money required of an affected individual to avoid identity theft can be enormous and especially onerous on students who are frequently on a more limited income with little expertise in personal finance and consumer credit. "

income with little expertise in personal finance and consumer credit.

For example, in 2008, security breach victims whose information was misused spent an average of 58 hours and $739 in out-of-pocket expenses in order to repair existing bank accounts damaged by identity theft.[63] These expenses include: postage, photocopying, purchasing police reports, travel, buying court records, and childcare.[64] When the security incident involved a new account that was fraudulently opened in the victim's name, victims spent an average of 165 hours and $951 dollars to resolve the fraud.[65]

Even more concerning is that it is very difficult to ever get fraudulent items cleared from a credit report. Even after expending significant effort, many individuals report that the fraudulent items continue to appear. The two most common reasons given by individuals to explain why they have been unable to clear their names are that, "credit agencies keep putting incorrect information back on my reports" (30 percent), and "my accounts keep getting sold to new collection agencies even though they have been cleared" (28 percent).[66]

Making matters worse, individuals may face severe consequences if they fail to clear negative and fraudulent items from their credit reports. For example, 23 percent of respondents in one survey indicated that being an identity theft victim affects their ability to get a job, and 5 percent in the same survey claimed to have lost their job as a result.[67]

Table of Potential Costs to Affected Individuals

Direct Costs	Indirect Costs
Telephone and mail costs connected with clearing up the adverse impact of data breaches	Worry about/concern for identity theft
Potential credit monitoring	Time to monitor and correct credit reports
Potential credit repair consultant	Potential credit score and rating impact

Patients of university-run health clinics and medical centers face a greater exposure through data breaches as electronic medical records become more common. Victims of medical identity theft have reported being billed for services provided to those individuals illegally assuming their identity and even contacted by collection agencies about those services.[68] Many of these victims' medical records now include medical information from an imposter.[69] This information may impact the victims' ability to maintain or obtain new health insurance coverage because of restriction on alleged pre-existing conditions. Eleven percent of medical identity theft victims have already reported being denied health or life insurance for reasons that they cannot explain.[70]

Identity Theft

A major concern with data breaches is that they may lead to identity theft. Identity theft is a form of fraud in which someone uses and assumes another person's personally identifying information, such as another person's name, social security number, or credit card number, without the other's permission, typically in order to access resources or obtain credit and other benefits in that person's name.[71] Identity theft

IMPORTANT POINT

"The prevalence of identity theft is serious, as the FTC estimates that as many as 9 million Americans have their identities stolen each year. It has been estimated that 1 in every 10 U.S. consumers has already been victimized by identity theft."

CHAPTER 1: DATA BREACHES ON CAMPUS

is an issue that continues to plague consumers, businesses, and law enforcement agencies. The prevalence of identity theft is serious, as the FTC estimates that as many as 9 million Americans have their identities stolen each year.[72] It has been estimated that 1 in every 10 U.S. consumers has already been victimized by identity theft.[73]

Identity theft crimes can take many forms, ranging from obtaining a credit card[74] to renting an apartment in someone else's name. Skilled thieves use a variety of methods to obtain such information, including dumpster diving (sorting through trash), phishing (fraudulent emails attempting to acquire sensitive information), changing another person's address, pretexting (manipulating people into divulging confidential information), and old-fashioned stealing.[75]

It is difficult to predict how long the effects of identity theft may linger. That is because it depends on many factors including the type of theft, whether the thief sold or passed information on to other thieves, whether the thief is caught, and problems relating to correcting a credit report.[76] Therefore, victims of identity theft should vigilantly monitor financial statements and credit reports for several months after discovering the crime, to stay alert for any other signs of identity theft.

Federal Trade Commission (FTC)

According to a report done by the Federal Trade Commission (FTC), identity theft is not always detectable by the individual victims,[77] since some many may not review their credit reports[78] or credit card statements vigilantly, and may not realize they are victims of identity theft until contacted by a debt collector. In addition, frequently the causes of identity theft are not known, making it more difficult to determine a remedy to an unknown cause.[79] The extended length of time to discover misuse greatly impacts the repercussions of such identity theft. Approximately 38-48 percent of victims discover someone has stolen their identity within three months, while 9-18 percent of victims do not learn that their identity has been stolen for four or more years.[80] Therefore, the difficulty and delay in realizing that someone is a victim of identity theft, can exacerbate the remedial efforts and costs associated with identity theft.

Resolving the issues and problems surrounding an identity theft is not only timely, and bothersome, but also costly. It can take up to 5,840 hours to correct the damage from ID theft, depending on the severity of the case.[81] The average victim spends 330 hours repairing the damage, which may include measures such as switching credit card companies, contacting multiple agencies such as law enforcement, financial institutions and credit bureaus to inform them about the fraud.[82] Furthermore, on average, it has been estimated that victims lose between $851 to $1378 out-of-pocket trying to resolve identity theft.[83] In addition, the median value of goods and services obtained by identity thieves was around $500, according to an FTC report.[84]

QUICK FACTS ON IDENTITY THEFT

1. Amount of time for identity theft victims to discover their identity has been stolen:

   - 3 months for approximately 38-48 percent of victims

   - 4 or more years for 9-18 percent of victims

2. Depending on the severity of the case, it can take up to 5,840 hours to correct the damage from ID theft.

3. The average victim spends 330 hours repairing the damage from ID theft.

4. On average, out of pocket costs for victims of ID theft range from an estimated $851 to $1378.

5. The median value of goods and services obtained by identity thieves is around $500.

In an effort to reduce the likelihood of identity theft, the FTC has issued a set of regulations that are called the Red Flags Rule.[85] The Red Flags Rule were developed by the FTC because the Fair and Accurate Credit Transactions Act[86] (FACTA) directed the FTC to promulgate regulations to mitigate the risk of identity theft. The concept behind the rules – and conveyed in the name – is that a company would train employees to recognize and respond to certain "red flags" that were indicators of potential identity theft.

CHAPTER 1: DATA BREACHES ON CAMPUS

The regulations that the FTC produced have been controversial. While they were finalized in November 2007, the FTC has delayed enforcement of the rules several times. In 2010, Congress stepped in to clarify its intention with the Red Flag Program Clarification Act of 2010. While these rules do not directly relate to securing personal information, administrators should monitor the evolution of the regulations because they do concern policies protecting an individual's information.

Conclusion

Colleges and universities are particularly vulnerable to data breach incidents, through intentional means such as malicious attacks or theft, as well as through accidental exposure or loss of data. Such institutions house vast amounts of sensitive data on hundreds of thousands of individuals, including alumni, current students, university hospital patients, administration personnel, and professors. The resulting costs in the case of a data breach can be considerable. Both the direct monetary costs incurred in containing the breach and notifying potentially affected individuals as well as the indirect costs of negative publicity and poor public relations may be burdensome. The cost incurred by affected individuals is also often onerous and may lead to further negative publicity for the college or university or ongoing liability from potential lawsuits against the college or university. Knowing what policies to put in place beforehand and how to best respond in the event of a suspected breach may help to mitigate the potential disastrous harm of such a loss of sensitive or personally identifiable information.

CHAPTER TWO

RECENT TRENDS IN DATA SECURITY LITIGATION AND REGULATORY ENFORCEMENT

Introduction

Litigation and regulatory enforcement arising from breaches of information security systems and procedures are legion and seemingly ever-growing. Moreover, given the nature and volume of information obtained by educational institutions, those entities are likely targets for claims arising from the release of sensitive information.

Consequently, would-be plaintiffs may base their claims not only on prior case law and legal theories, but they now have a complex patchwork of statutes on which to potentially measure a school's security compliance and liability. Individual consumer plaintiffs have had difficulty so far succeeding in court. This is because the basis for their claims typically requires the individual to prove that they suffered some sort of financial harm. Merely the concern or worry about identity theft is insufficient. However, when credit card data is involved in a breach the bank that has issued the lost card may have a significantly better chance of proving financial harm because of the expenses associated with reissuing credit cards. While the subject of data security litigation and regulatory enforcement could easily fill volumes of books, this chapter will briefly discuss the general theories of potential liability and review certain cases that provide guidance for universities and colleges.

Generally, there are three likely parties to bring a case based upon a breach of information security:

1. Federal government agencies

2. State government agencies and attorneys general; and

3. Private plaintiffs (or some combination of the three).

Federal Government Agencies

The federal agency most likely to bring an action is the Federal Trade Commission (FTC). The FTC may bring actions under a number of different statutes including the Federal Trade Commission Act,[87] the Gramm-Leach Bliley Act[88] (with respect to compliance with the Safeguards Rule), and the Fair Credit Reporting Act.

Federal Trade Commission Act

The FTC Act is a broad consumer protection law that makes "[u]nfair methods of competition in or affecting commerce, and unfair or deceptive acts or practices in or affecting commerce" unlawful.[89] For our purposes, the focus is on the words *unfair or deceptive* as these provide the basis for much of the FTC's enforcement with respect to privacy and information security.

Key to FTC enforcement are those three words above – *unfair or deceptive* – as they apply to an organization's privacy and security behavior. The FTC initially began enforcement against organizations for failing to fulfill promises in privacy policies. The FTC said that this was deceptive.

A representation, omission or practice is considered deceptive if it is likely to (1) mislead consumers who act reasonably or (2) affect consumers' behavior or decisions about the product or service. For example, if a university made certain public assurances of how it would manage individuals' personal information – via a privacy policy – but in fact treated the information differently, that might be the basis of a deceptiveness claim: saying one thing and doing another.

> **IMPORTANT POINT**
>
> "The FTC has more recently started to enforce information security practices, distinct from privacy practices which deal more with consumer notice and consent."

The FTC has more recently started to enforce information security practices, distinct from privacy practices which deal more with consumer notice and consent. The FTC initiated enforcement actions against organizations that have potentially applied inadequate security protections on personal information within their control. For these cases, which often arise from a security breach, the FTC has claimed that the organization's handling of consumer data was unfair. An act or practice is unfair if the injury it causes or is likely to cause is substantial, not outweighed by other benefits to consumers or competition, and not reasonably avoidable to consumers.[90] For a college or university that has suffered a data security loss, the question would follow the lines of "was the harm to consumers outweighed by what the cost would have been to implement better security practices?"

FTC Enforcement

Enforcement by the FTC typically involves a temporary restraining order or preliminary or permanent injunctions for alleged violations. While the FTC is active in prosecuting cases involving privacy concerns, most cases resolve by way of a consent order wherein the subject entity agrees to monitoring and controls imposed by the FTC.

For data security settlements, the FTC typically requires that the organization agree to development and monitoring of a comprehensive information security program. Usually these requirements involve:

1. Appointing leadership (and accountability) for the data security program within the organization

2. Conducting a risk assessment so that the organization documents the data it collects and the technological and non-technological risks to that information

3. Preparing and implementing comprehensive, written policies to safeguard the information

4. Appropriate steps to select and retain service providers that may be collecting and handling personal information for the institution

5. Regularly monitoring and re-evaluating the information security program so that the program evolves as the organization's business, data, and risk profile change.[91]

CHAPTER 2: RECENT TRENDS IN DATA SECURITY LITIGATION AND REGULATORY ENFORCEMENT

While these are the sort of safeguards that an information security program should encompass, the FTC consent orders usually include requirements of third party data security assessments and reporting to the FTC for a 20-year period.

FTC Prosecutions

The FTC has prosecuted actions against entities involved in education, although these have not yet raised data security issues. While the FTC has not yet enforced data security compliance against higher education, the fact that the FTC has prosecuted privacy faults puts higher education on notice that security enforcement is a possibility.

For example, *In the Matter of The National Research Center for College and University Admissions, Inc.*[92] the FTC alleged that the National Research Center engaged in deceptive practices by making misrepresentations regarding how and to whom personally identifiable information would be disclosed, and who funded the research that was done on the data that was collected. Ultimately, the National Research Center was required to make certain privacy disclosures, give notice of certain practices and not make certain misrepresentations.

Similarly, in another case, the FTC also challenged changes to the privacy policy of Gateway Training & Learning Center (an organization providing private tutoring and corporate training programs) which the FTC believed to be "material changes." Specifically, the FTC contended that Gateway Learning had promised in its privacy policy not to share personally identifiable information with third parties unless the consumer provided express consent but nevertheless shared such information without the required consent.

Further, the policy offered the consumer the right to opt-out of the sharing of information if the policy changed in the future. However, Gateway Learning changed its policy without providing consumers the opportunity to opt-out. The case resolved by way of a consent order which did not admit liability but did subject Gateway Learning to higher reporting standards and restrictions on its ability to change its privacy policy.[93]

Health Insurance Portability and Accountability Act (HIPAA)

> **IMPORTANT POINT**
>
> "a college or university may come under HIPAA to the extent it operates an academic medical center, hospital or health clinic and/or has health related information as part of research programs."

Given the current state of the health care reform debate, the Health Insurance Portability and Accountability Act (HIPAA) has gained a great deal of attention. HIPAA governs the use and disclosure of protected health information through the imposition of privacy, security, marketing and reporting requirements. While protected "individually identifiable health information" is generally not contained in educational or employment records,[94] a college or university may come under HIPAA to the extent it operates an academic medical center, hospital or health clinic and/or has health related information as part of research programs.

Litigation under HIPAA has been rare as courts have consistently held that there is no private right of action under the law.[95] This means that an individual patient does not have the right to file a lawsuit on the basis of a privacy or security violation. However, in 2009, as part of the federal government's economic stimulus package, HIPAA was amended to – among other things – expand enforcement authority to state attorneys general.

Electronic Communications Privacy Act (ECPA) and Computer Fraud and Abuse Act (CFAA)

Given the prevalence of computers and the data which is transmitted and stored on them, educational institutions should be aware of the Electronic Communications Privacy Act[96] (ECPA) and the Computer Fraud and Abuse Act[97] (CFAA). Both these statutes are frequently the basis of litigation.

The ECPA regulates when electronic communications can be monitored or reviewed by third-parties, such as a college or university providing Internet and email services to employees and students. It is a crime to intercept or procure electronic communications (including e-mail and other electronic transmissions and communications) unless certain exceptions apply.[98]

The CFAA provides both civil and criminal liability for any intentional access to computers or computer system which is unauthorized and results in damage to the system and/or the obtaining of a thing of value. Further, the CFAA provides for liability for the knowing transmission of a program, code or command that intentionally damages a protected computer, accesses a protected computer and recklessly causes damage, or accesses a protected computer without authorization and causes resulting damage.[99]

Potential exposure for educational institutions exists under both the ECPA and CFAA if the school is monitoring electronic systems and equipment used by students, employees and/or the public and gathering data from that monitoring. In the case of the CFAA, schools may be able to assert claims under the statute if its computers and/or systems are accessed without authority and thereby compromised.

State Government Agencies and Attorneys General

State government agencies and particularly state attorneys general may seek to enforce certain federal laws in addition to state information protection laws, such as those covering identity theft laws and electronic data and computer abuse provisions. As mentioned above, recent changes to HIPAA (the federal law addressing health information) and federal consumer financial protection laws have increased the opportunities for state attorneys general to prosecute federal claims.

State Attorney General Enforcement: Case Study

In January 2010, soon after the HITECH amendments came into effect, the Connecticut Attorney General Don Blumenthal filed suit against Health Net of Connecticut, which had reportedly lost a computer disk in May 2007. The lawsuit alleged that the health insurer failed to secure private information for roughly 446,000 enrollees and that the company failed to comply with its own policies regarding the protection of personal information; failed to effectively train and supervise its workforce on the proper policies for maintaining, using, and disclosing personal health information; and failed to encrypt the private information.

Six months later, the Connecticut AG announced a settlement that reportedly includes a $250,000 payment to the State of Connecticut as well as a "Corrective Action Plan" in which Health Net is implementing several detailed measures to protect health information and other private data in compliance with HIPAA. This plan includes continued identity theft protection, improved systems controls, improved management and oversight structures, improved training and awareness for its employees, and improved incentives, monitoring, and reports.

As demonstrated by the Connecticut Attorney General, enforcement by state agencies for data security failings may be on the rise. While state attorneys general have collaborated on the larger data security and privacy cases, there are many examples of state officials enforcing laws on their own. Because this is still a relatively new area of consumer protection, however, enforcement by state authorities has been limited to date.

Private Sector Plaintiffs

Finally, there are private sector plaintiffs. While the most obvious potential claimant against an institution would be a student or loan guarantor (parent) whose personal information was lost or stolen, this group has had difficulty establishing the economic harm or damages typically required to win a negligence case.

IMPORTANT POINT

"While the most obvious potential claimant against an institution would be a student or loan guarantor (parent) whose personal information was lost or stolen, this group has had difficulty establishing the economic harm or damages typically required to win a negligence case."

However, as alluded to above, in the case of banks that have had to issue new cards to replace those affected by a school's data incident, it is substantially easier to demonstrate damages.

The Problem of Damages in Private Actions

It is important to note that the mere violation of privacy laws does not equate to a successful claim. Rather, a plaintiff must establish that he or she has been damaged by the alleged breach – and that is often times very difficult to prove. This is frequently shown in cases where an individual contends that a security breach has resulted in the compromise of their private information which might render them susceptible to identity theft. Several courts have found that such claims do not present viable causes of action because the claim for damages was speculative.[100]

> **IMPORTANT POINT**
>
> **"It is important to note that the mere violation of privacy laws does not equate to a successful claim. Rather, a plaintiff must establish that he or she has been damaged by the alleged breach – and that is often times very difficult to prove."**

While individual consumers may have difficulty establishing any sort of out-of-pocket harm or damages, in circumstances involving the loss of credit cards colleges and universities have more reason for concern. There are two reasons for this: the fact that banks issuing credit cards spend money to re-issue them, and state laws concerning retailer liability in the event of a data breach.

What are the Payment Card Industry Data Security Standards?

The Payment Card Industry Data Security Standards (PCI DSS)[101] are a set of security measures that are imposed by the major credit card brands (for example, Visa, MasterCard, American Express, Discover) upon any entity that accepts credit cards for payment. These security requirements are incorporated within an institution's credit card processing contract between the school and its bank. Failure to properly protect credit card data can lead to higher fees, penalties, and potentially the inability to accept credit cards for payment.

The concern for any schools that accept credit cards – whether for payment of fees or transactions through school retail stores – is that laws imposing credit card liability to the organization that suffered the breach may spread to other states. California, New Jersey, Massachusetts and Texas have each considered these rules, which would require reimbursement of the expenses that banks incur when they must re-issue cards after an incident. In January 2010, Nevada updated its data protection law to mandate that all businesses in the state that accept payment cards be compliant with the PCI DSS.[102]

While consumers are typically protected from any fraudulent charges on cards, financial institutions that issue credit and debit cards often take a series of steps to protect their cardholders in the event of a data security breach. For example, financial institutions may cancel and replace the cards, close affected accounts and stop pending transactions, issue refunds or credits to cover the costs of unauthorized transactions, and notify cardholders affected by the breach. In all, it is relatively easy to imagine an average cost per card of $30, which contributes to significant sums if a university has had a data breach impacting, say, 5,000 individuals.

Private Action (Consumer Plaintiff): Case Study

One of the highest profile cases involving higher education has been *Guin v Brazos Higher Education Services Corp.*, a 2006 decision from Minnesota that involved a laptop stolen from an employee's home. In this case, the court found no negligence on the part of the Brazos Higher Education Service Corporation, a non-profit that originates and services student loans. Brazos had an employee whose company laptop was stolen from home.

The laptop was not recovered and the employee had not kept records of what databases (all unencrypted) might have been on the laptop. The company notified all 550,000 customers, advising some that personal information may have been accessed. One of the customers notified was Guin, who filed an action for negligence and other claims, even though there was no indication that a third party had accessed Guin's personal information.

In analyzing the claim for negligence and breach of duty, Guin argued that Gramm-Leach-Bliley created a statutory based duty for Brazos to protect the security and confidentiality of customers' nonpublic personal information, and that failure to do so was negligence. However, the court found no evidence that Brazos had failed to comply with the requirements of the GLB Safeguards Rule, and while the personal information was unencrypted, there was no GLB requirement for encryption. Furthermore, the court concluded that the theft of the laptop was not reasonably foreseeable.

Examples of State Laws Granting Private Right of Action for Credit Card Plaintiffs

Washington

Under a Washington State law effective July 1, 2010,[103] certain entities involved in credit card transactions may find themselves liable to financial institutions for costs associated with reissuing payment cards after a security breach. Fortunately for most colleges and universities, the threshold requires that the organization process at least six million transactions per year before potentially being liable; those with fewer annual transactions would not be covered by the law. The Washington law follows a May 2007 law enacted in Minnesota that codifies one aspect of the Payment Card Industry Data Security Standards (PCI DSS).[104]

Minnesota

The Minnesota law prohibits merchants (those accepting credit and debit cards for payment) from retaining credit or debit card security code data, PIN verification codes, or the full contents of any track of magnetic stripe data for more than 48 hours after the authorization of the transaction. Merchants are also strictly liable for costs incurred by financial institutions who assist consumers following the discovery of a security breach. While the data retention provisions were effective in August 2007, the retailer liability provisions became effective on August 1, 2008.

There are particular requirements in the PCI DSS that can help to reduce the likelihood or impact of a loss involving payment cards:

1. Beyond understanding the general requirements of the PCI DSS, pay particular attention to the security of payment card data that the institution holds and verify that the school is not retaining more data than allowed.

2. Because so many organizations engage third party processors to manage payment card transactions, verify that each processor is on the approved list maintained on the PCI Security Standards Council website.

3. Ensure that your institution's PCI compliance team has adequate resources or support, as the costs for remediating breaches are usually much larger than the costs for getting it right in the first place.

PART II:

WHAT FEDERAL & STATE LAWS APPLY TO SECURING DATA?

CHAPTER THREE

THE GRAMM-LEACH-BLILEY SAFEGUARDS RULE

Introduction

Colleges and universities collect personal financial information in the course of administering loans and other contexts. The FTC regulates how non-bank organizations must secure this personal financial information through the Gramm-Leach-Bliley Safeguards Rule. The Safeguards Rule describes how this information must be protected.

The Gramm-Leach-Bliley Act or GLB was finalized in 1999 as part of a substantial reorganization of how financial institutions operate and how financial services are regulated. A component of GLB concerns privacy notices and security safeguards associated with the personal financial information that any organization providing financial services must abide by.

This chapter focuses on the data security requirements imposed by the FTC over personal financial information in certain contexts. The FTC issued two rules under its GLB authority: the Privacy Rule[105] and the Safeguards Rule.[106] The Privacy Rule addresses communications with consumers in the form of privacy notices and governs what disclosures an entity may make. The Safeguards Rule is distinct in that it requires particular security measures be applied to personal financial information. While the Privacy Rule is not applicable to educational institutions complying with the Family Educational Rights and Privacy Act (FERPA), the Safeguards Rule remains directly relevant.

Privacy Rule

Through the Gramm-Leach-Bliley Act,[107] the FTC has jurisdiction over non-bank organizations that are significantly engaged in certain financial activities, which in turn makes these organizations "financial institutions" in the eyes of the regulators. While a college or university may not consider itself to be a financial institution, activities such as managing loan applications, granting loans, and potentially administering loans to students, parents or even employees are but one area in which institutions perform financial services-type activities.

In the Privacy Rule, the FTC discussed at length the criteria for being deemed a financial institution – largely the types of financial services described in the preceding paragraph. During the comment period, before issuance of the final rule, the FTC received several comments from colleges and universities requesting that they be excluded from the definition of financial institution and thus coverage of the regulation.

The Commission responded that "[t]he Commission disagrees with those commenters who suggested that colleges and universities are not financial institutions. Many, if not all, such institutions appear to be significantly engaged in lending funds to consumers. However, such entities are subject to stringent privacy protections in… [FERPA]…, which govern the privacy of educational records, including financial aid records. The Commission has noted in its final rule, therefore, that institutions of higher education that are complying with FERPA to protect records will be deemed to be in compliance with the Commission's rule."[108] This statement limits the application of the FTC's Privacy Rule, so that educational institutions are not obliged to comply with both.

Safeguards Rule

> **IMPORTANT POINT**
>
> **"The Safeguards Rule outlines a series of data security measures that an organization subject to the rule – including higher education – must apply in order to protect the personal financial information under its control."**

In notable contrast, the Safeguards Rule, issued two years later and setting forth security requirements with respect to consumer financial information, makes no such exception for compliance with FERPA, which has non-disclosure obligations but no equivalent safeguards requirements. Therefore, institutions complying with FERPA's confidentiality requirements are deemed compliant with the FTC's Privacy Rule, but compliance with the Safeguards Rule remains.

The Safeguards Rule outlines a series of data security measures that an organization subject to the rule – including higher education – must apply in order to protect the personal financial information under its control. These include data security measures that typically incorporate administrative (policies, training), technical (technology) and physical (locks on doors and cabinets) components to protect the information at issue.

In the Safeguards Rule, the FTC was directed by the underlying statute to develop standards intended to: "Ensure the security and confidentiality of customer records and information, protect against any anticipated threats or hazards to the security or integrity of such records; and protect against unauthorized access to or use of such records or information that could result in substantial harm or inconvenience to any customer."[109]

Because of the potential sensitivity and value of personal financial information, a combination of administrative, technical, and physical measures will be required to meet the requirements of the Safeguards Rule as well as to meet or exceed good practice.[110]

In establishing the safeguards, the FTC understood that these rules would apply to a wide variety of entities and a wide variety of industry sectors. Therefore, it was the intention of the FTC that in requiring any information security program that there be certain basic elements to ensure that the information security program addresses relevant aspect of operation while also maintaining flexibility for the entity that is being regulated.

As indicated above, the Safeguards Rule sets forth standards for developing, implementing, and maintaining reasonable administrative, technical and physical safeguards to protect the security, confidentiality, and integrity of customer information. The FTC safeguards rule applies to all customer information (meaning student, parent, and according to the FTC, employee information) that a university or college may hold regardless of whether the information relates to students or employees or applicants or any other relationship that may exist between the institution and the individual.

Purpose and Scope of the Safeguards Rule

The Safeguards Rule itself is relatively short, comprising only a single page in the Federal Register. We have stated the purpose of the rule earlier – to wit: implementing those sections of the Gramm-Leach-Bliley Act that set forth standards for developing, implementing and maintaining reasonable administrative, technical and physical safeguards to protect the security, confidentiality, and integrity of customer information.[111]

The scope of the Safeguards Rule is broad. It applies to all organizations subject to the FTC's jurisdiction and all customer information (as those terms are defined) in the organization's possession, "regardless of whether such information pertains to individuals with whom you have a customer relationship, or pertains to the customers of other financial institutions that have provided such information to you."[112] The application to higher education, then, is sweeping, in that anything falling within the definition of "customer information" must be protected in accordance with the Safeguards Rule, regardless of whether the information came from a student or parent, was generated by the institution in association with a loan review, or was simply provided by a third party lender verifying certain information.

Key Definitions from the Privacy Rule Applicable to the Safeguards Rule

Some familiarity with the FTC's Privacy Rule is helpful simply because terminology from the Privacy Rule is used in the Safeguards Rule. Generally, there are a few key definitions for our purposes.

Key Definitions from the Privacy Rule Applicable to the Safeguards Rule

Customer information means "any record containing non-public personal information ... about a customer of a financial institution."

Information Security Program is defined as "the administrative, technical, or physical safeguards you use to access, collect, distribute, process, protect, store, use, transmit, dispose of, or otherwise handle customer information."

Service provider means "any person or entity that receives, maintains, processes, or otherwise is permitted access to customer information through its provision of services directly to a financial institution that is subject to this part."[113]

Non-Public Personal Information means:

"(i) personally identifiable financial information; and

(ii) any list, description, or other grouping of consumers (and publicly available information pertaining to them) that is derived using any personally identifiable financial information that is not publicly available."[114]

Personally Identifiable Financial Information is any information:

A consumer provides to you to obtain a financial product or service from you;

About a consumer resulting from any transaction involving a financial product or service between you and a consumer; or

---

CHAPTER 3: THE GRAMM-LEACH-BLILEY SAFEGUARDS RULE

> You otherwise obtain about a consumer in connection with providing a financial product or service to that consumer.[115]

Translating the legalese from the regulations to a college or university context, the school collects personally identifiable financial information in many contexts. These may include loan subsidies to faculty and staff, loan and grant applications from students, supporting documentation from guarantors, and related information received from third parties such as credit reporting agencies conveying consumer credit scores. This becomes "customer information" when a student, parent, or employee engage in a loan or grant transaction through the school, even if the school is only a facilitating party and not the eventual lender. Even though the school may not be issuing the loan or grant, it is sufficient to be a part of the chain, holding that non-public personal information.

As we consider the definitions above, it is important to keep in mind the scope of the Safeguards Rule and specifically that these definitions and provisions apply even if the customer information was not provided directly to the institution by an individual. Note also that the definition of customer information is not limited to electronic data, so that information in any format is covered. Even though most information is generated and stored electronically, recent enforcement by the FTC and other federal agencies has included the improper disposal of hardcopy containing sensitive personal information.

The definition of information security program is also broadly applied. The FTC requires that an institution covered by the GLB Safeguards Rule must develop and maintain an information security program that goes beyond simple documentation to include training and awareness, technology measures, and audit and compliance mechanisms. We will go into further detail of what such an information security program might contain in the chapter Protecting An Institution's Information.

Standards for Safeguarding Student Financial Information

The Safeguards Rule sets forth the basic expectations – the Standards – and then provides additional detail – the Elements – of what are required for proper implementation of the standards.

Standards

The Safeguards Rule requires that each organization develops, implements, and maintains a comprehensive information security program that is written in one or more readily accessible parts and contains administrative, technical, and physical safeguards.

> **IMPORTANT POINT**
>
> "The Safeguards Rule requires that each organization develops, implements, and maintains a comprehensive information security program that is written in one or more readily accessible parts and contains administrative, technical, and physical safeguards."

Breaking this into its constituent parts, an organization must first develop a comprehensive, written information security program. Note that while the program need not be in a single document, it must be written and the reference is to a program and not simply to a policy. While a policy comprises part of the documentation, a program involves procedures to follow the policy, training, compliance monitoring and the like.

After developing the program – agreeing internally on its components – the Safeguards Rule requires that the documentation actually be implemented. Training and awareness, compliance monitoring, and audit should be familiar tasks, as if one were rolling out any other compliance policies across the school. The scope of these policies must cover the three aspects of information security safeguards: administrative (documentation, training), technical (technology), and physical (doors, locks), each of which is discussed in more detail in chapter 6 Protecting An Institution's Information.

The final requirement identified above (after development and implementation of the program) is that the organization should regularly assess the continued validity of the program documentation and update it as appropriate. As an educational institution collects or stops collecting certain personal identifiers, as the regulatory landscape changes, or as data incidents result in real or potential losses, it is important to regularly reassess whether the comprehensive program still matches the institutional needs. It is also important to have a sense of proportion, in that these programs must be appropriate to the size and complexity of the organization, the nature and scope the institution's activities, and the sensitivity of the customer information.[116]

This comprehensive information security program must be oriented toward ensuring the security and confidentiality of customer information, be the "customers" students, parents or employees; protecting against any anticipated threats or hazards to the security or integrity of this information; and protecting against unauthorized access to or use of such information that could result in substantial harm or inconvenience to any customer.[117]

Elements

The FTC goes on to identify a series of elements that are required for any information security program. Specifically at a minimum any information security program must designate an employee or employees to coordinate the information security program, and conduct a risk assessment to identify reasonably foreseeable internal and external risks to the security, confidentiality and integrity of the customer information. A risk assessment is best started with an understanding of what sort of information the institution holds, and then determining how harm might come to the information.

At a minimum this means that a risk assessment should cover each relevant area of an institution's operations, including employee training and management; information systems, including network and software design, as well as information processing, storage, transmission and disposal; and detecting, preventing and responding to attacks, intrusions or other failures. This last aspect – incident response – is a critical part of any program, as these days it is unwise to ask "if" an event will occur but rather "when" an event will occur.

In addition to designating an employee responsible for the information security program and conducting a risk assessment, an institution must design and implement safeguards to control the risks that were identified in the risk assessment above. Examples of risks that schools may experience are the improper disposal of documents with sensitive information, external hackers seeking entry to data within loan applications, rogue employees selling secreted information, accidental web posting of data due to the improper separate of computer systems, or inadequate employment or contractor background checks, especially for those with responsibilities for sensitive information. This will involve regularly testing or otherwise monitoring the effectiveness of these controls, much as any audit program would, to verify that the goals of the program are being achieved.

> **IMPORTANT POINT**
>
> "An institution must oversee its service providers by taking reasonable steps to select and retain those vendors capable of maintaining appropriate safeguards over the information as well as negotiating suitable contracts to ensure implementation and maintenance of these safeguards."

Each of these components of the comprehensive information security program should be found within the information security policies and procedures that an institution's IT and Information Security department is already doing. Verifying this, and making it an integral part of an institution's overall compliance effort, will be important if the program is to succeed and if the organization is to improve its compliance with the Safeguards Rule.

Service Providers and Outsourcing

Finally, because so many institutions outsource various functions, ranging from IT services to employee payroll to HR functions and Finance and Accounting, the FTC Safeguards Rule expressly addressed the role of these service providers. The definition of service provider means that if an institution is sharing employee data with a payroll processer or credit card data with a credit card processer or any other customer information, the institution will be responsible for confirming that the data is protected in accordance with the requirements of the Rule.

An institution must oversee its service providers by taking reasonable steps to select and retain those vendors capable of maintaining appropriate safeguards over the information as well as negotiating suitable contracts to ensure implementation and maintenance of these safeguards. Service providers may be responsible for a wide range of information produced by or prepared for a school. Simply within the scope of the GLB Safeguards Rule, these may include third party administrators of loan and grant applications, credit history providers, archiving and remote storage of physical files and electronic backups, as well as third parties hosting certain university computer systems.

GLB Safeguards Rule Checklist

Develop a comprehensive, written security policy containing:

- √ Administrative (policy) requirements
- √ Technical (technology) measures
- √ Physical (doors and locks) measures
- √ Review the documentation regularly and after any data security incident
- √ Require and implement regular training on the policies and associated details
- √ Engage internal or external resources to verify that the security program is effective
- √ Enforce the policy rules consistently

CHAPTER FOUR

STATE AND FEDERAL LAWS ON SOCIAL SECURITY NUMBERS

When one thinks of identity theft, valuable data toward building of a false profile, or the focus of state breach notification requirements, social security numbers or SSNs are invariably mentioned. While this federal identifier is now rarely used in education as a primary or secondary identifier for students, collection of SSNs is needed for employees (payroll and tax) and for loan applications. The sensitivity of this single identifier, however, means that an institution must take particular care.

The risk associated with the use of SSNs by higher education was highlighted in a data security article titled *University Databases In the Bull's Eye: Recent wave of university hacks nationwide exposes vestiges of former practice of using social security number as identifiers.*[118] While the news story focused on a breach from the University of Hawaii Manoa affecting approximately 53,000 students, faculty and other customers of the university's parking facilities, it reflects risk on the part of educational institutions that continue to retain SSNs. Even though virtually all institutions have ceased repurposing SSNs as student identifiers, the data often remains on many systems.

State laws increasingly mandate the protection of SSNs and reasonably prohibit use of them as identifiers. Concurrently, state legislatures have begun to take the lead away from federal regulators in the detailed prescription of how sensitive personal information such as SSNs, payment card data, and other information must be protected.

> **IMPORTANT POINT**
>
> **"As ubiquitous personal identifiers, SSNs have become valuable targets for identify thieves. SSNs are the required key to unlocking significant personally identifiable information on individuals."**

Social security numbers (SSNs) were first issued in 1936. Since that time, SSNs have become widely used as a type of national identification number. In 1961, the Internal Revenue Service started using SSNs as taxpayer identification numbers. Financial institutions have long used SSNs to verify the identity of their customers, check credit histories, etc. By law, banks and other financial institutions must track customers under customer identification programs, which requires the collection of SSNs. As ubiquitous personal identifiers, SSNs have become valuable targets for identify thieves. SSNs are the required key to unlocking significant personally identifiable information on individuals. As a result, federal laws and several state laws have been passed in an effort to enhance protection of SSNs and reduce the risk of identity theft through unauthorized acquisition of SSNs.

FPCO View of SSNs

The Family Policy Compliance Office (FPCO) within the Department of Education has responsibility for enforcing FERPA. Under FERPA and FPCO regulations, education records include two categories of information: directory and non-directory information. Directory information may generally be shared without the prior consent of the student and typically includes name, school email address, major, attendance dates, sports participation, degrees and honors, and photo. Non-directory information may not be shared without the student's prior consent, except in limited situations. This includes date of birth, ethnicity and gender, SSNs, grades, test scores, and grade point average.[119]

Amendments to the FERPA regulations have clarified that although a student identifier may be considered directory information, a student identifier will be non-directory information if it involves a student's SSNs.[120] The upshot of this is that the FPCO dissuades institutions from using SSNs as a student identifier.

Judicial View of SSNs under FERPA

In addition to the FPCO, courts have held that disclosure of SSNs would violate FERPA. In *Krebs v. Rutgers*,[121] the court held that SSNs were "personally identifiable information" covered under FERPA. Rutgers conceded that a policy of disseminating class rosters with SSNs would violate FERPA. The school contended it did not have a general policy of publishing SSNs, but only did so in isolated situations which did not constitute a "policy or practice" under FERPA. Rutgers had advised teachers not to post grades with SSNs, but did not provide similar guidance regarding class rosters. Although Rutgers did not have a stated policy of using SSNs with class rosters, "many occurrences" of doing so constituted a "practice" in violation of FERPA. Evidence of a single instance of using SSNs with posting of grades did not, however, result in a violation of FERPA. The court also noted that printing SSNs on school identification cards could be a violation of FERPA under some circumstances if the use did not serve a "legitimate educational interest."

Privacy Act of 1974

The Privacy Act of 1974 also limits the use of SSNs by federally funded institutions. Under the Privacy Act, a government agency cannot "deny to any individual any right, benefit, or privilege provided by law because of such individual's refusal to disclose his social security account number." The law also requires agencies to provide a SSN disclosure notice, stating whether or not disclosure is mandatory or voluntary and what uses will be made of the SSN.

Institutional Response to the Use of SSNs

In light of the recent attention to the risks associated with SSNs, several institutions have stopped using or have limited the use of SSNs for identification purposes. For example, Columbia University has adopted a policy that "the use of the SSN as a primary identifier shall be avoided, except as required by law or as required by the business necessity."[122] The school's policy is to "discontinue the collection of SSN except where necessary for employment records, financial aid

> **IMPORTANT POINT**
>
> **"In light of the recent attention to the risks associated with SSNs, several institutions have stopped using or have limited the use of SSNs for identification purposes."**

records, health records and other business and governmental transactions as required by law or to satisfy a business requirement."[123]

In its place, the school uses a nine digit Unique Person Number (UPN). To the extent SSNs are collected as permitted by the policy for business or legal reasons, the numbers must be "protected" and "secure."[124] In light of recent privacy law developments and best practices, such protection and security should be provided by using industry standard encryption technology for the electronic storage and transmission of SSNs.

State Responses to Use of SSNs

Several states have enacted laws restricting their use. First among these was California, with other states mirroring its requirements. Generally, these laws prohibit:

1. displaying SSNs publicly;
2. printing SSNs on cards used to access products or services;
3. printing SSNs on materials mailed to individuals; and
4. requiring individuals to transmit their SSNs unencrypted over the internet.

Most states, however, include exceptions for adherence to state and federal laws. In general, states may also enforce civil penalties for violations of these laws, and in some cases allow private causes of action.

The table in the Appendix includes a list of those states with laws that generally restrict the use of SSNs by both postsecondary institutions and other entities.

Additionally, some states have enacted laws specifically related to the use of SSNs by postsecondary institutions. In general, these laws prohibit:

1. using an SSN as a student's or employee's identifying number,
2. printing SSNs on identification or services cards, and

3. publicly displaying a student's SSN. However, broader restrictions may also apply, such as in Colorado, where postsecondary institutions must take "reasonable and prudent" steps to ensure the privacy of their students SSNs.

Generally, these prohibitions apply to *public* postsecondary institutions, but some states also apply them to *private* institutions. Further, at least two states, Oregon and Rhode Island, allow a student to recover damages and attorney's fees from public institutions that improperly disclose a student's SSN.

> **IMPORTANT POINT**
>
> **"Generally, these laws prohibit: (applicable to postsecondary institutions and other entities)**
>
> **1. displaying SSNs publicly;**
>
> **2. printing SSNs on cards used to access products or services;**
>
> **3. printing SSNs on materials mailed to individuals; and**
>
> **4. requiring individuals to transmit their SSNs unencrypted over the internet."**

Laws Specifically Relating to the Use of SSNs by Postsecondary Institutions

	Prohibition on using SSN as identifying number?	Prohibition on displaying SSN on identification card or other documents?	Other Information	Statutes
Arizona	Yes	Yes	Applicable to students in public institutions.	Ariz. Rev. Stat. Ann. § 15-1823

CHAPTER 4: STATE AND FEDERAL LAWS ON SOCIAL SECURITY NUMBERS

	Prohibition on using SSN as identifying number?	Prohibition on displaying SSN on identification card or other documents?	Other Information	Statutes
Arkansas	No	Yes	Applicable to students and employees in both public and private institutions. May not make SSN readable through magnetic strip or other encoded information on identification card.	Ark. Code Ann. § 6-61-128
Colorado	Yes	No	Applicable to students in both public and private institutions. Must take reasonable and prudent steps to ensure the privacy of a student's SSN. Approved institutions may phase out the use of SSNs.	Colo. Rev. Stat. Ann. § 23-5-127

	Prohibition on using SSN as identifying number?	Prohibition on display-ing SSN on identifica-tion card or other documents?	Other Information	Statutes
Illinois	No	Yes	Applicable to following public institutions: The University of Illinois, Southern Illinois University, Chicago State University, Eastern Illinois University, Governors State University, Illinois State University, Northeastern Illinois University, Western Illinois University, and community colleges. May not provide SSN or other personal information to businesses or financial institutions that issue credit cards, unless the student is 21 years of age or older.	110 Ill. Comp. Stat. 305/30; 110 Ill. Comp. Stat. 520/16; 110 Ill. Comp. Stat. 660/5-12; 110 Ill. Comp. Stat. 665/10-125; 110 Ill. Comp. Stat. 670/15-125; 110 Ill. Comp. Stat. 675/20-130; 110 Ill. Comp. Stat. 680/25-125; 110 Ill. Comp. Stat. 680/30-135; 110 Ill. Comp. Stat. 690/35-130; 110 Ill. Comp. Stat. 805/3-60
Kansas	Yes	Yes	Applicable to students and employees in both public and private institutions. May not encode an SSN into an identification card.	Kan. Stat. § 76-768
Kentucky	Yes	No	Applicable to students in public institutions.	Ky. Rev. Stat. Ann. § 164.283

CHAPTER 4: STATE AND FEDERAL LAWS ON SOCIAL SECURITY NUMBERS   53

	Prohibition on using SSN as identifying number?	Prohibition on display-ing SSN on identifica-tion card or other documents?	Other Information	Statutes
Maryland	No	Yes	Applicable to students and employees in public institutions.	Md. Code Ann., Educ. § 15-110
New Jersey	Yes	Yes	Applicable to students in both public and private institutions. Exemption where other state or federal law applies.	N.J. Stat. Ann. § 18A:3-28
New York	Yes	Yes	Applicable to students in both public and private institutions. Exemption where specifically authorized by law.	N.Y. Educ. Law § 2-b
Oregon	No	Yes	Applicable to students in public institutions. With certain exceptions, may not disclose SSN of an attending student. Student who suffers ascertainable losses from a violation may bring action to recover actual damages and may be awarded reasonable attorney fees.	Or. Rev. Stat. §§ 326.587–.591

	Prohibition on using SSN as identifying number?	Prohibition on display-ing SSN on identifica-tion card or other documents?	Other Information	Statutes
Rhode Island	Yes	Yes	Applicable to "individuals" in public institutions. May not for any purpose publicly display any four or more consecutive digits of an individual's SSN. In a civil action resulting from a violation, the Court may award damages, reasonable attorney fees, costs, and injunctive relief. Use of SSN not prohibited where required by law.	R.I. Gen. Laws. § 16-38-5.1
Virginia	No	Yes	Applicable to students and employees in public institutions. Exception for universities and colleges that have in place a prevention plan for the misuse of personal information. SSNs of donors or prospective donors are excluded from disclosure under the Freedom of Information Act, but disclosure is authorized at the custodian's discretion where not prohibited by law.	Va. Code Ann. §§ 2.2-3800, -3705.4.

CHAPTER 4: STATE AND FEDERAL LAWS ON SOCIAL SECURITY NUMBERS

	Prohibition on using SSN as identifying number?	Prohibition on display-ing SSN on identifica-tion card or other documents?	Other Information	Statutes
Washington	Yes	No	Applicable to students and employees in both public and private institutions.

Exemption for SSN used for identification purposes related to employment, financial aid, research, assess-ment, accountability, transcripts, or other otherwise required by state or federal law. | Wash. Rev. Code § 28B.10.042 |
| West Virginia | Yes | Yes | Applicable to students in both public and private institutions.

Exemption for student identification cards, directories or similar listings produced before July 1, 2002.

May not use SSN for internal record keeping purposes or studies. | W. Va. Code § 18-2-5f |
| Wisconsin | Yes | No | Applicable to students in both public and private institutions.

Disclosure of SSN allowed if required by a federal or state agency or private organization in order for the institution or the student to participate in a particular program. | Wis. Stat. § 36.32 |

This table does not include the list of states with laws that prohibit the use of SSNs in general, for both postsecondary Institutions and other entities.
Courtesy of Foley & Lardner, LLP

CHAPTER FIVE

STATE BREACH NOTIFICATION LAWS

Major breaches like the Veterans Affairs breach or that of BJ's Wholesale underscore why 46 states, the District of Columbia, Puerto Rico, the US Virgin Islands, and New York City[125] have all enacted breach notification legislation.

The First Data Breach Notification Law

In 2002, the California Senate introduced SB 1386, which became the first data breach notification law.[126] Prior to 2002, individuals did not have a right to know if their personal information in the possession of a company had been compromised. The bill came about as a result of an incident involving a state data center, where computer hackers accessed the personal information of approximately 265,000 state workers. Although the breach occurred in early April 2002, and was discovered in early May 2002, affected employees were not notified until May 21, 2002. The intention of SB 1386 was to provide consumers a greater opportunity to protect their financial security by requiring organizations that keep consumer personal information in a computerized data system to quickly disclose to those consumers any breach of the security of the system.

Many States Soon Followed California's Lead

Several state legislatures attempted to follow California's lead in 2003 and 2004, however the breach notification bills that were introduced failed to pass. The landscape changed following the ChoicePoint breach in February 2005. That breach compromised the personal information of more than 163,000 consumers across numerous states, and several state Attorneys General expressed outrage over the company's plan to only notify affected consumers in California, the only jurisdiction requiring notification by law. As a result, by the end of 2005, 22 states had passed legislation.

Today, 46 states have passed data breach notification laws, as well as the District of Columbia, Puerto Rico, the U.S. Virgin Islands, and New York City. While many of these laws appear similar on the surface, there are nuances that must be appreciated by an organization creating an incident response plan. Organizations must determine the scope of the law, what obligations arise under the laws, as well as the consequences for non-compliance.

Who is Covered under State Data Breach Notification Laws?

Data breach notification laws generally apply to persons or businesses that own, license or maintain certain types of information. Some laws are further restricted to persons or businesses who conduct business in the state. Thus, where the law is not restricted to organizations that conduct business within the state, out-of-state organizations may have to comply with other states' laws if they own, maintain or license personal information of those states' residents.

The "persons", "businesses" or "entities" that the notification obligations apply to vary among state laws, and often the definitions comprise a laundry list of organizations, including almost every entity imaginable. A few states opted to use other terms of art in describing who the law applies to, for example: information brokers, data collectors, and database owners.

Applying Your Existing Notification Procedures

Some laws take into account that organizations may have notice obligations pursuant to already established security programs or other federal or state laws, regulations or guidelines. In those states, the organization is either exempt from the law entirely, or there is a provision deeming those organizations to be in compliance with the breach notification law as long as notice is provided to the affected individuals in accordance with those legal or internal notification procedures.

For example, in California, a "person or business that maintains its own notification procedures as part of an information security policy for the treatment of personal information and is otherwise consistent with the timing requirements of [the law], shall be deemed to be in compliance with the notification requirements . . . if the person or business notifies subject persons in accordance with its policies in the event of a breach. . ."[127]

What Information is Covered Under State Data Breach Notification Laws?

Notification obligations are triggered by a breach of personal information. Personal information is generally defined as an individual's first name or initial and last name, in combination with any one or more of:

1. a social security number,

2. a state identification card number or drivers license, or

3. a financial account number or credit or debit card number along with any required security code, access code or password that would permit access to such account.

Some states, such as North Dakota, have broadened this definition to include medical information, biometrics, other forms of state and employer information, or mother's maiden name.

Information is generally not considered personal where it is lawfully made publicly available through government records or the media. Most states also provide that when the information is secured by some method rendering the data unreadable or unusable, it is not personal information, and thus, notification obligations do not arise under the laws. Most states, the exceptions being Wyoming and the District of Columbia, specifically name encryption as the method of securing this information. Fewer states, but Wyoming[128] among them, use redaction as the method of securing the information. And fewer jurisdictions yet, do not name a particular method of securing the

> **IMPORTANT POINT**
>
> "When a security breach occurs, all of the laws require the organization to provide notice of the breach to affected residents. A handful of states require notification of affected out-of-state individuals as well, including Hawaii, New Hampshire, North Carolina, and Wisconsin."

data, as long as the end result is that the information is unreadable or unusable, for example, in the District of Columbia.[129]

What is Required Under State Data Breach Notification Laws?

A security breach is typically defined in the laws as the unauthorized access to or acquisition of computerized data that compromises the security, confidentiality or integrity of personal information. Not all jurisdictions limit security breaches to computerized data; breaches of paper documents also trigger notification requirements in Alaska, Hawaii, Indiana, Massachusetts, North Carolina, and Wisconsin. Some of the state laws only require notification in the case of "material" breaches, where, for example, there has been a material compromise of security, confidentiality or integrity, or where harm to the consumers (e.g. identity theft, loss or injury) is caused or reasonably believed to have been caused.

A security breach typically has not occurred where the unauthorized acquisition was caused by an employee who acted in good faith, and there has been no further subsequent unauthorized access or acquisition, except in Connecticut and Puerto Rico. Nebraska and Ohio also created an exception for disclosures pursuant to a search warrant, subpoena, or other legal authority.

Residents and Non-Residents

When a security breach occurs, all of the laws require the organization to provide notice of the breach to affected residents. A handful of states require notification of affected out-of-state individuals as well, including Hawaii,[130] New Hampshire,[131] North Carolina,[132] and Wisconsin.[133]

Additional Notices

In some states and in some circumstances, to provide warning of a potential influx of consumer concerns, organizations must also notify the Attorney General, another regulator, or consumer reporting agencies. Montana requires notification to a consumer reporting agency for every breach; most other states only require notification to a consumer reporting agency where a certain number of individuals are affected. Massachusetts requires notice to the Attorney General and the director of the Office of Consumer Affairs and Business Regulation regardless of the number of residents affected.

Risk of Harm Factor

Some laws provide for circumstances where notification is not required. Where the laws mandate that an investigation be conducted, either by the organization or by law enforcement agencies, notification is sometimes not required where the results of the investigation lead to a conclusion that there is no likelihood of harm or the misuse of personal information is not reasonably likely or possible. Delaware,[134] Louisiana,[135] and New Jersey[136] are examples of laws that contain this sort of exemption. Keep in mind that where an organization determines that notification is not required, it is prudent to document such a determination and maintain records to that effect for at least five years.[137]

Timing of Notification

Notification to affected individuals must be made in the most expedient time possible and/or without unreasonable delay, to comply with the majority of the laws. Florida,[138] Ohio,[139] and Wisconsin[140] require that notice be made within 45 days following discovery of a breach. The California Office of Privacy Protection recommends a best practice of notifying individuals within ten days of discovering a data breach.[141]

CHAPTER 5: STATE BREACH NOTIFICATION LAWS

The laws enumerate circumstances when delaying notification is reasonable, the most common ones being to accommodate the legitimate needs of law enforcement and to take measures that determine the scope of the breach and restore reasonable integrity to the breached system. The only states that do not provide a delay to determine the scope of the breach or restore integrity to a system are Massachusetts, New Hampshire, and Wisconsin.

Notification by Vendors

When organizations do not own or license the personal information that has been breached, the breached organization must notify the owner or licensor of the data. There is a great deal of variation and flexibility among the laws of when notification must be made to data owners, however the most common timing requirement is to provide notice "immediately after discovery" of a breach. To help data owners fulfill notification obligations, some states require that vendors cooperate with the owner or licensee and/or share information relevant to the breach.

Contents of Notification Letters

Although not specified in many states, a handful of laws detail what should be included in notification letters to affected individuals. Organizations drafting a template notification letter may wish to consider the following provisions.

Provisions to Consider for Template Notification Letter

Details around the incident, such as:

- A description of the nature of the breach;[142]

- The approximate date of the breach;

- The approximate number of affected individuals;[143]

- The types of personal information affected by the breach;

- The general acts of the business to protect personal information from further unauthorized access;
- An estimate of the time and cost required to rectify the situation;
- Whether criminal complaints have been filed.

Contact information of:

- The organization, including a telephone number;
- Consumer reporting agencies;
- The Federal Trade Commission (FTC); and
- The state Attorney General.

Information for individuals to mitigate harms, such as:

- The right to obtain a police report;
- How to place a fraud alert;
- How to place a security freeze;
- Remaining vigilant by reviewing account statements and monitoring credit reports;
- Reporting suspected incidents of identity theft to law enforcement; and
- Obtaining information about how to avoid identity theft from the FTC.

It is wise, however, for each jurisdiction in which there is a notice obligation to check the website of, for example, the state Attorney General, as there may be specific forms or guidance provided that identify the particular information that is required for notice to either consumers or to the state agency. Massachusetts has these forms available, and is also unique in that it requires that very little detail of the incident be provided in the consumer notification.

> **IMPORTANT POINT**
>
> *"in most cases, the ability to provide notification by e-mail is limited by other prerequisites"*

Individual Notice via Mail or Email

In every jurisdiction, providing notice in writing or by mail is acceptable. E-mail notification is also an acceptable form of notification; every law with the exception of Wisconsin[144] has an explicit provision for e-mail notification. However, in most cases, the ability to provide notification by e-mail is limited by other prerequisites such as:

1. using e-mail as the primary method of communication with the recipient;

2. being consistent with the Electronic Signatures in Global and National Commerce Act;[145] or

3. the business being primarily operated on the internet. Other less prevalent methods of providing notice include by telephone or by fax.

When Is Substitute Notice Permissible?

All state laws also provide circumstances where a substituted form of notification may be provided. There are three factors that are often determinative of whether substitute notice is available for an organization who experienced a data breach: 1) the number of people affected, a state-dependent threshold ranging from 1,000 to 500,000 people; 2) the cost of providing notice, another state-dependent threshold ranging from $5,000 to $250,000; or 3) if the entity does not have sufficient contact information to provide traditional methods of notice.

Methods of Substitute Notice

The methods of providing substitute notice include, where possible, all of the following means: e-mail notice, posting a notice on the organization's website and providing disclosure to media. The scope of the media to be involved is generally major state-wide media, however in some states, regional or local media may need to be involved. Having covered the who's, when's and how's of notification, next we must explore what happens when notification is not provided or provided in a manner that does not comport with the laws.

Who Enforces the Law and What are the Consequences of Non-Compliance?

Well over half of the data breach notification laws are enforced by the state Attorney General. Otherwise, the law is enforced by the department that handles consumer protection or affairs, or in a few cases, the insurance or banking regulator. These agencies generally can pursue injunctions[146] and/or monetary penalties against organizations that do not comply with their notification obligations under the laws. The bigger concern for most organizations is likely the fines for non-compliance.

Civil Penalties for Noncompliance

Civil penalties under the laws range from $100 to $150,000 per violation. It is unclear in some states whether "per violation" means per individual affected or per security breach incident, regardless of the number of individuals affected. However, many states provide a "per violation" penalty as well as a maximum penalty, suggesting that violations are assessed on a "per individual" basis, for example if you fail to notify 10 individuals that were required to be notified, that would constitute 10 violations. Providing a maximum is to cap the penalty in the case of egregious breaches involving hundreds or thousands of affected people. For example, Alaska provides that the penalty for violations will be $500 for each state resident who was not notified, up to a maximum of $50,000.[147] In jurisdictions where a minimum per violation amount is set, the enforcing agency could take into account the elapsed time since the breach was discovered in assessing the fines to be levied, as long as the total remains under any statutorily established maximums.

> **IMPORTANT POINT**
>
> "Organizations that are non-compliant also face the possibility of individuals exercising a private right of action. Several jurisdictions either allow private rights of action or do not impair a resident's ability to pursue civil remedies when injured as a result of an organization's failure to notify."

Instead of penalizing organizations based on the number of violations, Florida and Ohio assess penalties starting from the 46th day after the breach was discovered and the amount is based on the time elapsed. These penalties start at $1,000 per day the breach remains undisclosed beyond the 45 days, up to $10,000 in Ohio if the breach is not disclosed within 90 days and up to $500,000 in Florida when it passes the 180 day mark.[148]

Litigation After Noncompliance

Organizations that are non-compliant also face the possibility of individuals exercising a private right of action. Several jurisdictions either allow private rights of action or do not impair a resident's ability to pursue civil remedies when injured as a result of an organization's failure to notify. For example, in California "any customer injured by a violation of this title may institute a civil action to recover damages."[149] Other jurisdictions that allow for actions by citizens include Delaware,[150] the District of Columbia,[151] Hawaii,[152] Illinois,[153] Louisiana,[154] Maryland,[155] New Hampshire,[156] North Carolina,[157] Puerto Rico,[158] South Carolina,[159] Tennessee,[160] Virgin Islands,[161] Virginia,[162] and Washington.[163]

Conclusion

To avoid being found non-compliant and therefore be subjected to penalties, organizations must plan for a breach. With a written, detailed security incident response plan in place, the impact of a breach on the business and its employees and customers may be reduced. While this chapter has presented the key similarities and differences in the current breach notification laws, the law is constantly evolving and, as a result, it is important that whomever the organization appoints in charge of compliance also follows developments in the law.

Developments that should be followed include updates to the existing laws, the passing of other breach laws, and the introduction of more proactive security laws. Existing laws are being amended to create greater obligations on organizations. An example is Idaho HB161, although vetoed by the Governor, it had amended the Idaho Code §28-51-105 to require notification to the Attorney General. Moreover, states that currently do not have any data breach notification law are in the process of consideration (e.g. Kentucky HB553).

A new trend appears to be emerging among state legislatures requiring more proactive security protection from organizations. Several state laws already create obligations for organizations to safeguard information in their possession, however the Massachusetts data security regulation[164] and the Nevada encryption law[165] contain provisions with a greater degree of specificity than before, such as the obligation to encrypt data transmissions. Now, other states are following suit, such as Michigan[166] and Washington.[167] Organizations have to shift focus from a reactive posture, of ensuring plans are in place to respond to a breach, to a more proactive posture, preventing a breach from occurring in the first place.

CHAPTER 5: STATE BREACH NOTIFICATION LAWS

PROTECTING PERSONALLY IDENTIFIABLE INFORMATION:
A GUIDE FOR COLLEGE AND UNIVERSITY ADMINISTRATORS

PART III:

PRACTICAL STEPS TO PROTECT INFORMATION AND RESPOND TO BREACHES

CHAPTER SIX

PROTECTING AN INSTITUTION'S INFORMATION

Introduction

Securing information requires a combination of administrative tools like policies and training, physical tools like ID badges and locked doors, and technology tools such as encryption and antivirus software. The combination of these administrative, physical and technical safeguards means that security should be viewed as a process, rather than a technology or a product. While a technology like antivirus software is an important component of the effort, information security is fundamentally a combination of administrative, technical, and physical safeguards to help ensure the confidentiality and the integrity of the data in question.

- **Administrative safeguards are usually policies and procedures as well as training and awareness activities.**

> **IMPORTANT POINT**
>
> **"information security is fundamentally a combination of administrative, technical, and physical safeguards to help ensure the confidentiality and the integrity of the data in question."**

- Technical safeguards involve hardware and software to encrypt data and to protect the organization's computer network from internal and external threats.
- Physical safeguards include locks on buildings, doors, and filing cabinets, as well as closed circuit television (CCTV) cameras and other tools.

Each of these is an important component toward assuring that information is not shared beyond those who have a need to know (confidentiality) and that the information is not improperly modified or erased (integrity).

While administrative and physical safeguards are an import aspect of any security program, technology often receives greater visibility, and in some instances is better suited to counter specific risks. Because malware is so often surreptitiously loaded onto university computer systems – particularly laptops – numerous systems with access to the school's network may be infected. Software is better suited to monitor and prevent such intrusions, although the Verizon 2010 Data Breach Report indicated that organizations often have the information available about such infections but fail to review the relevant computer logs.

In this chapter, we will review the basics of these safeguards: administrative, technical and physical. It begins with an understanding of what data an institution wants to protect, because it is difficult to protect data if you do not know where the data is stored and where it goes; it is also important to understand precisely what data the institution has, because not all information is equally sensitive or worthy or protection. Identifying the information will lead toward categorizing the nature of the data and thus the type of safeguards appropriate, given the importance of the information.

Conduct a Risk Assessment

A risk assessment is a review of the data a school holds plus a review of the sensitivity of the information and the impact to the institution if the information were to be lost or improperly used or disclosed. The risk assessment subsequently informs an institution's administration of what sort of safeguards (and, indirectly, resources) should be applied to protect the information.

Identify all Relevant Information

The starting point of a risk assessment or information protection program is a data mapping project. While it is possible to complete this exercise with varying levels of detail or scrutiny, fundamentally an organization should identify all information residing within its environment or entrusted to a third party service provider. This latter point is important to keep in mind, as organizations of all types including higher education rely heavily on outsourced functions ranging from payroll to loan administration and from IT to accounting services.

The first step in this is to define the data in question. Certainly for colleges and universities the scope of information involves personal information and its various subsets of protected health information or financial data. Does the information involve trade secrets or intellectual property still in development at an academic medical center or the physics department of an engineering school? Or does the information include faculty applicant and recruit information along with the institution's five year strategy? Because different types of information are arguably of different "value" or "worth" to an institution and to an individual, it is helpful to understand how much of each type of data is within the school's control or responsibility. Dividing data by subsets may also be necessary – particularly with personal information – as regulations and requirements may vary by data type or the context in which the information is collected and used.

There is no single way to undertake a data mapping exercise, but the following examples will provide a head start.

Some Steps to Take in a Data Mapping Exercise

Review System Documentation

Understand the type of data that information systems are designed to collect.

Conduct Interviews

Speak with individuals in different roles to understand how they collect and process the information within the scope of the risk assessment; asking the same or similar questions of different stakeholders (say, Admissions, Financial Services, Health Services, and IT) may lead to different responses, as different functions within the school will have varying perspectives on what is collected, who has access, and how the data is protected.

Use Data Loss Prevention Technologies

A type of automated monitoring software to identify categories of information stored or used within a computer network

Check with System and Data Owners

Similar to the interviews suggested above, system and data owners may have different perspectives of what information is within the system, how it is used, and who has access to it than do the users of the system or the data.

Categorize the Information

Once a school has some level of confidence in what information is within the environment (beyond anecdotal reports), the next step is to categorize the information by impact level. That is, if the data were lost, became corrupted and unusable, or were misused, what would be the effect upon the institution. This impact or effect could be reflected in financial loss, legal damage or harm to the institution's reputation.

While the precise vocabulary will vary from one educational institution to another and in fact different schools or groups within a university may use different taxonomies, the simplest categories reflect low, moderate, and high impact levels. These might be reflected in terminology such as Public, Internal Use Only, Confidential & Proprietary, as but one example. Regardless of the wording, the following descriptions prepared by the National Institute of Standards and Technology (NIST) should provide good starting points for a school's own use.

NIST Descriptions for Categories of Information by Impact Level

---

Low Impact

The loss of confidentiality, integrity or availability could be expected to have a limited adverse effect on an institution's operations, assets, or individuals. If data is compromised, the organization is still able to perform its primary functions with a relatively minor impact upon finances, reputation or losses to individuals.

Moderate Impact

The loss of confidentiality, integrity or availability could be expect to have a serious adverse impact on the institution's operations, assets or individuals. This means that while the organization is able to perform its primary functions, effectiveness is significantly reduced. The effect includes significant damage to assets (whether computing systems, student information or financial data), financial loss, and potentially harm to individuals that does not involve loss of life or serious life threatening injuries.

High Impact

The loss of confidentiality, integrity or availability could be expected to have a severe or catastrophic adverse effect on the institutions operations, assets or individuals. The practical impact means that the institution is not able to perform one or more of its core functions.[168]

CHAPTER 6: PROTECTING AN INSTITUTION'S INFORMATION

The scope and wording of these examples should of course change to reflect the needs of each school and preferably across the community. The type of data and impact will vary from a rural college to an urban medical center to a physics lab performing sensitive research.

Having established the type of data within the environment and a framework for categorizing the data, the next step is to decide which factors to use for determining impact levels and then implementing the appropriate policy, procedures, and controls. As the team deliberates which category fits which data type, consider some of the factors below.

Sensitivity Factors When Categorizing Information

Identifiability

Determine how easy is it for someone to identify a specific individual based on the data in question. A social security number uniquely and directly identifies a person, while a telephone area code relates to a broad set of people.

Quantity of Information

Consider how much data is at stake. For example, both Admissions and Alumni Affairs collect and maintain significant files on individuals with varying levels of sensitivity.

Data Field Sensitivity

Evaluate the sensitivity of specific data fields within a broad set of records, so that an SSN or financial account number or other special types of information are considered.

Access to and Location of the Information

Distinguish between who needs access to the information versus who would like access to the information. There are significantly more opportunities to compromise

---

74   PROTECTING PERSONALLY IDENTIFIABLE INFORMATION:
A GUIDE FOR COLLEGE AND UNIVERSITY ADMINISTRATORS

data files when they are accessed more often or by more people. Also consider whether the information is normally transmitted or transported off-site.[169]

Apply Appropriate Safeguards

There is almost no end to the potential safeguards one could apply to protect information. One of the significant decisions that school administrators must confront is the balance between the sensitivity of the information, the impact of harm to the data, and available resources. An important consideration here is the concept of compensating controls; for example, the decision not to implement certain technical safeguards is deemed appropriate because of other administrative or policy safeguards that will be used instead. Also, in considering appropriate safeguards, keep in mind whether legal requirements apply or whether the information (such as some personal information) needs to have its confidentiality protected because it is already public information.

Administrative safeguards include the development of comprehensive policies and procedures, as described below.[170]

IMPORTANT POINT

"There is almost no end to the potential safeguards one could apply to protect information. One of the significant decisions that school administrators must confront is the balance between the sensitivity of the information, the impact of harm to the data, and available resources."

Administrative Safeguards

- Implement access rules to determine who may access particular files

- Put information retention schedules and procedures in place

- Set up incident response and data breach notification systems

- Ensure privacy and security aspects of software and information system development

- Minimize the collection, disclosure, sharing and use of the information

- Institute sanctions and other consequences for failing to follow privacy and security rules

- Create exception procedures to recognize and monitor appropriate exceptions to policies and procedures

- Develop proper contract wording for service providers with access to or responsibility for the information

- Develop an incident response plan

- Implement procedures to manage the transmission and sharing of data outside the institution, such as minimum security controls within recipient organizations

- De-identify personal information to the extent possible

- Engage the institution's compliance or audit team to monitor the effectiveness of the program

- Use technology to monitor and log access to data files and review those logs to determine if improper access is occurring

- Implement rules with respect to what types of information can or cannot be stored on portable devices, such as USB drives, iPhones, CDs and so forth

- Use encryption technology to protect specific categories of data while the data is not being used

- Require complicated passwords and require that passwords be modified on a regular basis

While this is a long list of points that could be included within a comprehensive set of policies and procedures, it does not reflect the full range of recommendations or potential steps that might be suitable for any particular organization. Which brings us to the importance of people in this effort. We have mentioned earlier the significance of engaging stakeholders across the institution, regardless of size, and this remains as important at the policy development and execution stage as it was when we mentioned it during data mapping. While technology is a significant tool to protect information, the success of an information protection program will largely succeed or fail because of the human factor.

Provide Employee Training and Awareness

Training and awareness are critical components of any information protection program. They help to mitigate the effects of social engineering, they help to achieve the mental buy-in of each employee, and they help to reinforce generally the value that the organization places on protecting the information in question.

Toward this end, it is important to understand the difference between training and awareness, and that each has a proper role.

The goal of training within an organization is to build knowledge and skills in a more formalized mechanism that enables a school's administration to track comprehension and enables administrators to monitor the completion of any course requirements. The privacy and security training for any individual will vary depending upon the role the person has

> **IMPORTANT POINT**
>
> **"The goal of training within an organization is to build knowledge and skills in a more formalized mechanism that enables a school's administration to track comprehension and enables administrators to monitor the completion of any course requirements."**

within the institution: financial services, health services, admissions, IT and counseling reflect some of the common roles, and there may be particular rules or requirements to be taught, depending on an individual's job or role. Fundamentally, privacy and security training would normally encompass the following information.

Information to Provide in Privacy and Security Training

- Definitions of the information in scope, such as personal information, and examples of how the data is used in context
- Applicable privacy laws, regulations, and policies
- Restrictions on data collection, storage, sharing and use
- Roles and responsibilities for protecting the information
- Guidance on how to dispose of or destroy the data
- Directions on how to use exceptions processes, to the extent they exist
- Sanctions for misuse of data or failing to conform to policy
- Directions for how to recognize a security incident and what to do in response
- Retention schedules[171]

IMPORTANT POINT

"While formal training is important, ongoing awareness efforts can sometimes be equally effective when the goal is to help people understand how privacy and security affects their role within the institution."

While formal training is important, ongoing awareness efforts can sometimes be equally effective when the goal is to help people understand how privacy and security affects their role within the institution. Awareness typically relies on less formal, more frequent attention-grabbing techniques like signs and poster campaigns, laminated reminders attached to computer monitors, and email newsletters.

This is not unlike the training and awareness the school may already have for sexual harassment or non-discrimination compliance. While much of the content may repeat what is within the formal training, the awareness component is a less formal way to convey updates to new scams that are being used to steal identities, providing updates on privacy items in the news, and examples of how employees have been held accountable or rewarded for protecting institutional information.

Data Management: Retention and Destruction Considerations

Overview

The management of data presents certain legal issues pertaining to the retention and destruction of data. A competent and consistently enforced document retention policy can help reduce an institution's risk by ensuring that electronic data is handled properly. Some organizations operate without any formalized plan for document retention and destruction. Others have policies in place but fail to include electronic data in their protocol. Either of these approaches increases risk to the institution and its information, regardless of whether it is personal information or evolving intellectual property.

IMPORTANT POINT

"A document retention policy formalizes an entity's protocol for saving and discarding documents received or created in the ordinary course of business. Such a policy may aid an organization in litigation when documents were properly destroyed pursuant to the plan in place; conversely, failure to enact a competent policy may undermine a position in litigation, and failure to protect information subject to discovery can have dire consequences."

CHAPTER 6: PROTECTING AN INSTITUTION'S INFORMATION

A document retention policy formalizes an entity's protocol for saving and discarding documents received or created in the ordinary course of business. Such a policy may aid an organization in litigation when documents were properly destroyed pursuant to the plan in place; conversely, failure to enact a competent policy may undermine a position in litigation, and failure to protect information subject to discovery can have dire consequences.[172] There are numerous situation in which an entity may face unnecessary consequences due to inadequate or improperly enforced document retention procedures. Evidence discovered in documents retained far longer than necessary may expose a company to unforeseen liability. A school may also haphazardly destroy documents that should have been retained, making it susceptible to claims of spoliation (destroying evidence) even when no intentional destruction of documents is alleged.

Document Retention Laws

When institutions operate without valid document retention policies, or fail to follow existing policies, they place themselves in a position of unnecessary risk for claims of spoliation. Failure to retain electronic data in the face of litigation may subject a party to monetary sanctions.[173] However, simply setting a document retention policy is not enough. The policy must be valid and consistent enforced.[174] Therefore, the risk of unnecessary liability or sanctions is substantially reduced if an organization's electronic documents are properly organized and maintained.

> **IMPORTANT POINT**
>
> **"the risk of unnecessary liability or sanctions is substantially reduced if an organization's electronic documents are properly organized and maintained."**

Tips for Avoiding Document Retention Disasters

School administrators and IT must work to ensure that their record retention and destruction processes comply with all applicable laws. The following provides measures entities can take to comply with the record retention requirements.

Steps to Take in Complying with Record Retention Requirements

Coordinate with IT

Coordinate with the technology department as they will be largely responsible for successful implementation.

Instill Accountability

Establish clear accountability for policy enforcement. While an executive-level employee may be responsible for overall enforcement, be sure the staff handling the daily procedures is educated about the importance of the policy and held accountable.

Train Your Staff

Teach employees how to manage their electronic data. While technology helps, one of the weakest links remains employees and contractors.

Conduct Self-Assessments

Audit your retention policy. It will be easier to argue your policy is reasonable if it is reexamined and any necessary adjustments are made on a regular basis.

Ensure Accuracy

The technology used by an organization for its electronic documents must result in a complete and accurate copy of the documents, including all exhibits, schedules, side letters, etc., that comprise the contract, and pages with any handwritten changes or notation.

No Editable Versions

An editable version of the document should not be used for the electronic copy. For example, a Word version of a document should not be used as the official electronic copy as such formats are typically editable.

CHAPTER 6: PROTECTING AN INSTITUTION'S INFORMATION

Understand Retention Periods

The electronic copy must remain accessible as long as legally required.

Index Files for Accessibility

The database should also provide an appropriate indexing and document management system to ensure that an entity's employees (or others who are authorized) are able to readily locate, view and print the electronic copy.

Apply Safeguards to Vendors

If any of the electronic information will be maintained outside of an entity's internal IT network and environment, strong contracts should be in place with each vendor having control over or access to an entity's electronic data. At a minimum, the contracts should address data privacy and security, backup, disaster recovery, warranties, service levels, availability of hosted applications and data, ownership of intellectual property and data, indemnification and termination transition services.

Have Effective Security Programs

An organization should ensure it has at least "industry standard" data security, backup and disaster recovery systems and procedures in place. If your school intends to rely heavily on electronic records, it is important to ensure those records are properly safeguarded against unauthorized access and destruction (security), and can be timely restored in the event the active electronic record is corrupted, destroyed or otherwise not readily available (backup and disaster recovery).

Privacy Impact Assessments

Overview

Once an institution has adopted the previously discussed guidance, there needs to be a mechanism to incorporate either changes to the information systems or new additions to the information system. A common way to do this is through the conduct of privacy impact assessments for electronic information systems.

Privacy Impact Assessments are practical methods of evaluating privacy in information systems and collections, and documented assurances that privacy issues have been identified and adequately addressed. Furthermore, Privacy Impact Assessments are structured processes for identifying and mitigating privacy and associated security risks.

For example, if a university is developing a student ID that can be used as a charge card that carries the school's branding and is usable only within the school's point of sale networks, what impact has this on privacy and security? What information is available on the card and how are limits and account access controlled? Where will the data be stored and how may similar or different rules for different data be leveraged for this new product?

Conducting a Privacy Impact Assessment ensures compliance with laws and regulations governing privacy and demonstrates an organization's commitment to protect the privacy of any personal information it might collect, store, retrieve, use and share. It is a comprehensive analysis of how the entity's electronic information systems and collections handle personally identifiable information.

The objective of the Privacy Impact Assessment is to systematically identify the risks and potential effects of collecting, maintaining, and disseminating personally identifiable information and to examine and evaluate alternative processes for handling information to mitigate potential privacy risks.

CHAPTER 6: PROTECTING AN INSTITUTION'S INFORMATION

Activities that NIST has Identified as Triggering a Privacy Impact Assessment

- Converting paper-based records to electronic systems.

- Applying new functions to existing information collection changes anonymous information into information in identifiable form.

- Using existing IT systems for new purposes including application of new technologies, significantly changes how information in identifiable form is managed in the system. (For example, when an entity employs new relational database technologies or web-based processing to access multiple data stores, such additions could create a more open environment and avenues for exposure of data that previously did not exist).

- Adopting or altering business processes so that databases holding information in identifiable form are merged, centralized, matched with other databases or otherwise significantly manipulated. (For example, when databases are merged to create one central source of information, such a link may aggregate data in ways that create privacy concerns not previously an issue).

- Applying new user-authenticating technology (e.g., password, digital certificate, biometric) to an electronic information system accessed by members of the public.

- Incorporating into existing information systems databases of new information in identifiable form purchased or obtained from commercial or public sources. (Merely querying such a source on an ad hoc basis using existing technology does not trigger the Privacy Impact Assessment requirement).

- Sharing functions between organizations may involve significant new uses or exchanges of information in identifiable form.

- Altering a business process that results in significant new uses or disclosures of information, including incorporation into the system of additional information in identifiable form.

- Adding new information in identifiable form to a collection and thus, raises the risks to personal privacy. (For example, the addition of health or financial information may lead to additional privacy concerns that otherwise would not arise). [175]

Conclusion

This chapter outlined a framework for protecting information. As a framework – or skeleton – it is applicable to all categories of information, whether the concern is a student's academic and financial records, employee information, or intellectual property that a professor is developing. It all begins with an understanding of what information the organization has, categorizing the different types of data, and apply suitable protections based on the sensitivity of the information.

Administrators within higher education will need to coordinate with different stakeholders through the steps above. The technology team will be an important component with respect to identifying the data held as well as where the data goes and what the "suitable" protections may be. The legal team and compliance or audit team should be involved regarding the document retention and destruction stages, and various departments will also have input on how to categorize appropriately the sensitivity of different information.

In the end, the protection of information, like so many other topics addressed in other chapters, will rely on cooperation across different stakeholders.

CHAPTER SEVEN

RESPONDING TO AN INCIDENT

Even when entities take concerted measures and follow guidance to prevent security breaches, there is no absolute way of preventing such breaches from occurring. As a result, a response plan is crucial. Given the ever increasing profile of security breaches – both in the eyes of the general public and regulatory bodies – it is imperative that the response plan be comprehensive, thoroughly and thoughtfully planned, yet capable of swift implementation.

> **IMPORTANT POINT**
>
> **"Given the ever increasing profile of security breaches – both in the eyes of the general public and regulatory bodies – it is imperative that the response plan be comprehensive, thoroughly and thoughtfully planned, yet capable of swift implementation."**

Moreover, entities must be prepared to juggle a number of competing considerations and concerns when responding to breach – ranging from legal compliance to public relations management. This chapter outlines recommended steps for entities to consider when responding to a breach – and preferably, even prior to an occurrence.

Do Not Wait. Have a Response Plan Ready

As with emergency preparations, the importance of having a response plan in advance cannot be understated. The only way the university could effectively marshal such resources is by having the equivalent of an emergency response plan prepared in advance. When faced with their first breach, entities almost uniformly underestimate the scope of the task lying ahead of them.

To stay ahead of the curve, entities should not only have a response plan ready but also assemble a team to implement and execute the plan. This response team should receive training to obtain deep knowledge regarding the entity's information and data handling practices and policies. Moreover, it is helpful for such individuals to be versed in the types of information that are stored; how they are stored; how long they are stored; and why they are stored.

Data Breach Case Study

UCLA had prepared for such a compromise in their system and immediately began instituting its security incident response policy. Administrators and IT staff removed the vulnerable server from the network and alerted the FBI.[176] A subsequent investigation revealed that the perpetrator had compromised the server more than a year earlier, in October, 2005, but had remained undetected the entire time even though the University had remained in full compliance with policies of University of California and UCLA governing security standards and procedures.[177] The malicious software was designed to not only infiltrate the server, but to also systematically expunge any digital footprints it might leave behind. As noted earlier in the 2010 Verizon report, one of the significant flaws in security defenses has been the failure to review audit logs thus reducing the chances of identifying most malicious software.

The investigation also confirmed the malicious nature of the intruder's activities. UCLA, similar to many of its sister University of California schools, had been subject to prior intrusions to their systems. Most of these unauthorized invasions turned out to have somewhat innocuous objectives such as using the server for personal storage of downloaded movies and music. The intent of the intrusion discovered in November, 2006, however, was to specifically gain access to individuals' personally identifiable information stored on the server.[178] Although the infiltrator had potential access to the entire database of more than 800,000 names, social security numbers, and contact information, later forensic analysis determined that only a significantly smaller subset of those names appeared to have been targeted.[179]

The nature of the attack left UCLA in a very difficult and costly position. Although only a small subset of the data appeared targeted, the University worried about exposure to liability from the 800,000-plus people whose data was compromised. UCLA officials struggled with whether or not to voluntarily notify all of the potentially exposed individuals even in cases where the exposure could not be confirmed; a potential logistical nightmare and massive economic undertaking.[180] The University decided, given the scope of potential legal liability of foregoing such notification, to provide notice to the larger group. The logistics of the task required the immediate launching of an information Website along with a call center operation that, at its height, had 1,600 operators in 26 locations.[181] The call center eventually processed almost 36,000 calls or 4.5% of those notified, while the Website provided information and guidance regarding the breach to 105,000 unique visitors.[182] The call procedure included a process for escalating dissatisfied consumers to a single, higher-level UCLA official. 600 people were forwarded through this escalation process, and of that number reportedly only five remained dissatisfied. As a practical matter, the ability of a school to effectively manage the frustrations and concerns of affected individuals will go a long way toward limiting longer term repercussions.

Forensic evidence eventually concluded that approximately 28,500 individuals' data may have been exposed. Even though UCLA officials ultimately declared that, as of March, 2007, the stolen personally identifiable information had not been used for fraudulent purposes, it had nonetheless spent significant time and resources investigating the attack and complying with applicable law.[183]

CHAPTER 7: RESPONDING TO AN INCIDENT

Entities often outsource aspects of their response. For example, the New York State Consumer Protection Board advises entities to consult with privacy professionals and attorneys in responding to incidents.[184] Furthermore, third-party vendors are increasingly offering "turn-key" services that provide data analytics, and logistical support in the form of mailings and call-support centers for affected individuals to contact. Additionally, public relations firms also offer crisis management services to manage the disclosure of the breach to the public at-large and field press inquiries. Even if a school chooses to outsource all or parts of its response, it is important that a response team and plan be nonetheless internally in place.

Given the widespread enactment of state laws requiring written notification of security breaches, the cornerstone of response plans will naturally be the preparation and dissemination of security breach notification letters to possibly affected individuals. A response plan should incorporate the following measures.

Requirements for a Response Plan

- Ascertain the nature of breach;

- Contain and control the breach and preserve data integrity;

- Involve and cooperate with law enforcement;

- Determine the scope and type of information compromised by the breach;

- Contact other entities if appropriate;

- Notify regulatory and other state agencies as required;

- Notify Credit Reporting Agencies if appropriate;

- Consider further assistance or support to affected individuals;

- Prepare notice letters;

- Set up a hotline to respond to inquiries from letter recipients and individuals who believe they may have been affected; and

- Note lessons learned for purposes of future responses.

Ascertaining the Nature of the Breach

When confronted with an incident, institutions should take immediate steps to ascertain the nature of the possible security breach. In other words, they should determine whether the possible breach of information arises from: hacking and unauthorized access of its network; theft of tangible property (such laptops, desktops, hard-drives; backup storage, optical storage media (such as CD-ROMs or DVD-Roms) or thumb drives; or mere misplacement of property containing data. In doing so, entities should exercise care in also establishing the date and time of loss, possible perpetrators, and witnesses. Furthermore, another key preliminary determination is whether or not the data in question was in encrypted form. This is because, under certain state laws, notification obligations are not-triggered when the compromised information was encrypted.

While the above may appear to be self-evident, entities sometimes are unaware that a breach has occurred until individuals begin contacting them to complain that they have recently been victims of identity theft. An inventory checklist is helpful in such instances to ascertain how and if a breach occurred. This step is also useful insofar as many states (with the notable exception of Massachusetts)[185] require that notification letters include a description of what occurred.

Contain and Control the Breach and Preserve Data Integrity

Once the nature or cause of the breach is ascertained, it is important to take immediate measures to assure that the breach is controlled and contained. In this part of the process, it is advisable to involve information technology personnel to assess how to best to do so in an effective and expedient manner. Many state Attorney General offices and consumer protection offices offer

> **IMPORTANT POINT**
>
> "Once the nature or cause of the breach is ascertained, it is important to take immediate measures to assure that the breach is controlled and contained."

guidance in instances where the breach arises from compromised computer systems. As just one example, the Vermont Attorney General suggests measures including:

- Isolating the affected system and possibly taking servers offline

- Activating auditing software

- Preserving system logs

- Making backup copies of data files believed to have been damaged or compromise, and securing these backups

- Identifying all systems and agencies connected to the compromised system.[186]

IMPORTANT POINT

"In cases involving theft or physical loss of equipment it is important to assess what information was contained in such hardware, and whether such information could potentially give an unauthorized individual access to secure networks and data files not residing in the lost or stolen hardware."

In cases involving theft or physical loss of equipment it is important to assess what information was contained in such hardware, and whether such information could potentially give an unauthorized individual access to secure networks and data files not residing in the lost or stolen hardware. If such is the case, steps should be taken to secure those networks and files by, for example, modifying secured access protocols.

IMPORTANT POINT

"Finally, given the possibility of investigation by law enforcement agencies, it is important that possible evidence be properly preserved and not tampered with. Specifically, an affected school or department should not, at this stage, delete or move any compromised data, or conduct forensic analysis without consultation with law enforcement."

Finally, given the possibility of investigation by law enforcement agencies, it is important that possible evidence be properly preserved and not tampered with. Specifically, an affected school or department should not, at this stage, delete or move any compromised data, or conduct forensic analysis without consultation with law enforcement.

Involve and Cooperate with Law Enforcement

One of the key steps to a successful response plan is proper cooperation with law enforcement agencies. When a breach involves illegal activity such as theft of property or unauthorized access to systems, an institution should contact law enforcement to report the incident, and fully cooperate with any criminal investigation.

The Federal Trade Commission also recommends that organizations contact law enforcement when the incident gives rise to the potential of identity theft.[187] Moreover, if local law enforcement is unfamiliar with handling and investigation of security breaches, the local office of the FBI or U.S. Secret Service should be contacted.[188] To assure continuity and no lapses in communication, designate an individual to be a point-of-contact for law enforcement.

> **IMPORTANT POINT**
>
> "if local law enforcement is unfamiliar with handling and investigation of security breaches, the local office of the FBI or U.S. Secret Service should be contacted."

> **IMPORTANT POINT**
>
> "In their cooperation efforts, campus officials should also fully educate law enforcement regarding their response plan. Specifically, even if no final determination has been made, the organization should apprise law enforcement that they are in the process of determining whether breach notification letters will be transmitted. This will give law enforcement the opportunity to offer input and possibly object to the timing of such notifications if they believe the letters will interfere with the investigation."

CHAPTER 7: RESPONDING TO AN INCIDENT

In their cooperation efforts, campus officials should also fully educate law enforcement regarding their response plan. Specifically, even if no final determination has been made, the organization should apprise law enforcement that they are in the process of determining whether breach notification letters will be transmitted. This will give law enforcement the opportunity to offer input and possibly object to the timing of such notifications if they believe the letters will interfere with the investigation.

If law enforcement asks for a delay, schools should request to be advised as to when they can provide breach notifications without impeding the criminal investigation. It is also advisable that the delay request be in writing. Alternatively, diligently document a delay request by, for example, noting the name of the law enforcement official, the name of the agency and the date of the request. Finally, it is important that constant communication and follow-up with law enforcement be maintained. The Vermont Attorney General, for example, requires that entities contact the responsible law enforcement officer every fifteen (15) days to determine if the requested delay is still required.

Determine the Scope and Type of Information Compromised by the Breach

Breach notifications are a product of the type of information that has been compromised. Therefore, entities must establish what type of information has been acquired or is reasonably believed to have been acquired, and analyze whether such information fits into the categories requiring notifications. Furthermore, given that different states have different requirements (*e.g.*, some states cover medical information) and definition of "notice-triggering information," one cannot overstate the importance of meticulously verifying all applicable state laws.

> **IMPORTANT POINT**
>
> "Breach notifications are a product of the type of information that has been compromised."

As a threshold matter, the determination as to whether the law of a particular state applies depends on whether any affected individuals reside or hold a physical address in that state. This determination will prove useful in the notifications themselves, as a majority of states (with the notable exception of Massachusetts) require that notifications to their residents provide a description of the categories of compromised information. Finally, it is again important to stress that different states establish different notice-triggering thresholds and also impose different obligations.

> **IMPORTANT POINT**
>
> **"If your school stores, houses or uses data from other entities (such as lending organizations), you should contact those entities. This is because these organizations may have their own separate response obligations under applicable law."**

Contact Other Entities if Necessary

If your school stores, houses or uses data from other entities (such as lending organizations), you should contact those entities. This is because these organizations may have their own separate response obligations under applicable law.

Notify State Agencies and Attorneys General as Required by State Laws

An increasing number of states require that state agencies including state attorney general offices and consumer protection agencies be notified of an incident prior to transmission of breach notification letters to affected individuals. For example, the State of New York requires that entities submit a "Security Breach Reporting Form" to the following three agencies:

1. the New York State Attorney General's Office;

2. the New York State Office of Cyber Security & Critical Infrastructure Coordination; and

3. the New York State Consumer Protection Board.

Beyond law enforcement, the affected individuals are to receive notice and mailed copies of security breach notifications.[189]

CHAPTER 7: RESPONDING TO AN INCIDENT

> **IMPORTANT POINT**
>
> "A majority of states require that Credit Reporting Agencies (CRAs) – such as Experian, Equifax, and TransUnion – be notified when a threshold number (which varies by state) of individuals are believed to be affected by the breach and will be sent breach notification letters."

Notify Credit Reporting Agencies if Appropriate.

A majority of states require that Credit Reporting Agencies (CRAs) – such as Experian, Equifax, and TransUnion – be notified when a threshold number (which varies by state) of individuals are believed to be affected by the breach and will be sent breach notification letters. Sch may contact the three major CRAs in the following manner:

- Equifax
  U.S. Consumer Services
  Equifax Information Services, LLC
  T: 678-795-7971
  Email: businessrecordssecurity@equifax.com

- Experian
  Experian Security Assistance
  P.O. Box 72
  Allen, TX 75013
  Email: BusinessRecordsVictimAssistance@experian.com

- TransUnion
  T: 1-800-372-8391
  Email: fvad@transunion.com

> **IMPORTANT POINT**
>
> "While not required by breach notification laws, many breach response plans include the provision of complimentary credit monitoring services to affected individuals."

Consider Further Assistance or Support to Affected Individuals

While not required by breach notification laws, many breach response plans include the provision of complimentary credit monitoring services to affected individuals. In 2008, the Connecticut Attorney General Credit chided Bank of New York's response to a security breach incident as woefully inadequate and specifically requested that it provide "two years of free credit monitoring, including $25,000 in identity theft insurance, as well as free credit freezes."[190] The inclusion of at least one year of credit monitoring is indeed becoming a standard component of security breach response plans. Experian, Equifax and TransUnion all provide credit monitoring services and, typically, such services also include "insurance."[191] Aside from offering protection to affected individuals, these measures are useful public relations tools that demonstrate institutional concern for affected individuals.

Preparing Notices

As initial matter, it is crucial to delineate and track the qualification criteria for recipients of notification notices. Doing so will prove helpful when individuals inquire as to why they have or have not received a notification. Furthermore, this is an important process for purposes of filtering out false-positives – *i.e.*, individuals who should not receive notifications yet receive them anyway. While it is important to make sure that the response plan covers all affected individuals, false-positives are problematic as they may unnecessarily propagate and heighten alarm over a breach.

Even in cases where a law enforcement agency requests that the notifications be delayed, entities should proceed with preparation of breach notification letters when required by law. This is especially important because certain states have begun requiring that notices be sent within a limited time frame from authorization by law enforcement. Maine is noteworthy as its law limits delay due to a law enforcement request to a maximum of seven business days.

Absent a law enforcement request, the overwhelming majority of states require that notification letters be sent expediently and without unreasonable delay. A number of states place even more stringent timing requirements. For example, the Vermont Attorney General Office requires that letters be sent within 10 business days

CHAPTER 7: RESPONDING TO AN INCIDENT   97

of discovery of a breach.[192] The California Office of Privacy Protection recommends that entities provide notifications within 10 business days of discovery of the breach.[193]

Content of Notices

Entities should once again note that different states impose different requirements as to the contents of letters. Generally, the majority of states require that notification letters contain the following information:

General Requirements for Notification Letters in the Majority of States

- A general description of the incident.

- A listing of the categories of personal information compromised.

- Steps taken to protect the compromised information from further unauthorized access.

- Steps that will be taken to assist affected individuals – including a toll-free helpline and information about free credit monitoring/insurance.

- Guidance as to how individuals can protect themselves (e.g., place fraud alerts, change access passwords to their financial accounts, review of credit reports, request issuance of new credit and debit cards), and contact information for the three major Credit Reporting Agencies – Experian, Equifax, and TransUnion.[194]

The notification letters should use simple, clear and concise language. A common complaint from recipients of such letters revolves around the over-use of legalese and technical language – rendering such letters almost unintelligible to a layperson. Moreover, institutions should avoid the temptation to adopt a one-size-fits-all approach in drafting their letters to residents of different states.

Massachusetts, for example, deviates from the majority of states as its law expressly prohibits that the letter provide details regarding the incident or that it list the categories of compromised information and number of affected residents. Additionally, certain states may place additional requirements such as the inclusion of information regarding requests for credit freezes. While states require that contact information for state agencies be included in notifications, the specific agencies and method of contact will vary from state to state.

> **IMPORTANT POINT**
>
> **"The notification letters should use simple, clear and concise language. A common complaint from recipients of such letters revolves around the overuse of legalese and technical language – rendering such letters almost unintelligible to a layperson."**

Delivery of Notices

Breach notification laws typically require that letters be sent to affected individuals via first-class mail. While most laws also allow for email notifications in certain cases, entities must take care in complying with federal and state laws governing such transmissions and assure that they have the necessary consent from the affected individuals. Alternatively, in specific instances usually linked to prohibitive costs, substitute notice, as provided by statute, may be appropriate provided that the threshold eligibility requirements are met. When transmitting notifications, entities should keep a log tracking the recipients and dates of transmission for purposes of future inquiries from individuals who believe they should have received a notification but did not receive one.

Set Up a Hotline to Respond to Inquiries from Letter Recipients and Individuals Who Believe They May Have Been Affected.

As part of the response plan, a toll-free telephone line should be established to field inquiries from individuals receiving notices as well other individuals expressing concerns that they may have been affected by the incident. For purposes of responding to individual inquiries, the preparation of "FAQ" will prove helpful in training response staff. Some frequently asked questions are listed below

---

FAQs from Individuals Who Have Been or May Have Been Affected by Data Breaches

- What happened?
- When did it happen?
- Why was I not notified sooner?
- What specific items of personal information were involved?
- What is being done regarding the breach?
- What measures have been taken to prevent this from happening again in the future?
- Are recipients of the notifications the victims of identity theft?
- What steps can be taken to determine whether or not the personal information has been used by somebody else?
- Do I have to pay for a credit report?
- What is a fraud alert?
- What should I do if I found out that I am the victim of identity theft?
- Should I obtain a credit freeze on my credit files?

Finally, given the increased attention security breaches have been receiving in the media, educational institutions should designate a point person to field inquiries from the media and state agencies.

> **IMPORTANT POINT**
>
> **"designate a point person to field inquiries from the media and state agencies"**

Note Lessons Learned for Purposes of Future Responses

Security breach responses are often protracted and unfailingly difficult processes. There undoubtedly will be mistakes made and steps, which in hindsight, could have been handled better. The construction of a knowledge base and formation of institutional knowledge are invaluable to prepare for future breaches. Therefore, each organization should take note of any missteps and readjust their plans accordingly.

APPENDIX

State Prohibitions on the Use of Social Security Numbers, Applicable to both Postsecondary Institutions and Other Entities.

	Prohibition on public display of SSNs?	Prohibition on printing SSNs on cards used to access products or services?	Prohibition on printing SSNs on materials mailed?	Prohibition on requiring the transmission of unencrypted SSNs over the internet?	Other Prohibitions?	Exemptions?	Statutory Enforcement?	Statutes
Alabama	No	No	No	No	N/A	N/A	N/A	
Alaska	Yes	Yes	Yes	Yes	Yes	Yes	Yes	Alaska Stat. §§ 45.400 to .480
Arizona	Yes	Yes	Yes	Yes	Yes	Yes	Yes	Ariz. Rev. Stat. Ann. §§ 44-1373 to 44-1373.03

	Prohibition on public display of SSNs?	Prohibition on printing SSNs on cards used to access products or services?	Prohibition on printing SSNs on materials mailed?	Prohibition on requiring the transmission of unencrypted SSNs over the internet?	Other Prohibitions?	Exemptions?	Statutory Enforcement?	Statutes
Arkansas	Yes	Yes	Yes	Yes	No	Yes	Yes	Ark. Code Ann. § 4-86-107
California	Yes	Yes	Yes	Yes	Yes	Yes	No	Cal. Civ. Code §§ 1798.85 to .89
Colorado	Yes	Yes	Yes	Yes	No	Yes	Yes	Colo. Rev. Stat. §§ 6-1-112, -113, -713.
Connecticut	Yes	Yes	Yes	Yes	No	Yes	Yes	Conn. Gen. Stat. Ann. § 42-470 [Pub. Act. No. 08-167 (effective Oct. 1, 2008)]
Delaware	No	No	No	No	N/A	N/A	N/A	

	Prohibition on public display of SSNs?	Prohibition on printing SSNs on cards used to access products or services?	Prohibition on printing SSNs on materials mailed?	Prohibition on requiring the transmission of unencrypted SSNs over the internet?	Other Prohibitions?	Exemptions?	Statutory Enforcement?	Statutes
District of Columbia	No	No	No	No	N/A	N/A	N/A	
Florida	No	No	No	No	N/A	N/A	N/A	
Georgia	Yes	No	No	Yes	No	Yes	No	Ga. Code. Ann. § 10-1-393.8
Hawaii	Yes	Yes	Yes	Yes	No	Yes	Yes	Haw. Rev. Stat. Ann. § 487J-2
Idaho	Yes	No	No	No	Yes	No	No	Idaho Code § 28-52-108(1)

APPENDIX

	Prohibition on public display of SSNs?	Prohibition on printing SSNs on cards used to access products or services?	Prohibition on printing SSNs on materials mailed?	Prohibition on requiring the transmission of unencrypted SSNs over the internet?	Other Prohibitions?	Exemptions?	Statutory Enforcement?	Statutes
Illinois	Yes	Yes	Yes	Yes	No	Yes	Yes	815 Ill. Comp. Stat. 505/2QQ
Indiana	No	No	No	No	N/A	N/A	N/A	
Iowa	No	No	No	No	N/A	N/A	N/A	
Kansas	No	No	No	No	N/A	N/A	N/A	
Kentucky	No	No	No	No	N/A	N/A	N/A	

	Prohibition on public display of SSNs?	Prohibition on printing SSNs on cards used to access products or services?	Prohibition on printing SSNs on materials mailed?	Prohibition on requiring the transmission of unencrypted SSNs over the internet?	Other Prohibitions?	Exemptions?	Statutory Enforcement?	Statutes
Louisiana	No	No	No	No	N/A	N/A	N/A	
Maine	No	Yes	No	Yes	Yes	Yes	Yes	Me. Rev. Stat. Ann., tit. 10 §§ 1272, 1272-B, 1273
Maryland	Yes	Yes	Yes	Yes	Yes	Yes	Yes	Md. Code Ann., Comm. Law §§ 13-401 to -411, 14-3402
Massachusetts	No	No	No	No	N/A	N/A	N/A	
Michigan	Yes	Yes	Yes	Yes	Yes	Yes	Yes	Mich. Comp. Laws Ann. §§ 445.82-445.86

APPENDIX

	Prohibition on public display of SSNs?	Prohibition on printing SSNs on cards used to access products or services?	Prohibition on printing SSNs on materials mailed?	Prohibition on requiring the transmission of unencrypted SSNs over the internet?	Other Prohibitions?	Exemptions?	Statutory Enforcement?	Statutes
Minnesota	Yes	Yes	Yes	Yes	Yes	Yes	No	Minn. Stat. Ann. §§ 325E.59 *There are proposed legislations to change the language of these provisions, including defining potential remedies and penalties.*
Mississippi	No	No	No	No	N/A	N/A	N/A	
Missouri	Yes	Yes	No	Yes	Yes	Yes	No	Mo. Ann. Stat. § 407.1355
Montana	No	No	No	No	N/A	N/A	N/A	
Nebraska	Yes	Yes	No	Yes	No	Yes	No	Neb. Rev. Stat. § 48-237 *(Prohibitions apply to employers)*

	Prohibition on public display of SSNs?	Prohibition on printing SSNs on cards used to access products or services?	Prohibition on printing SSNs on materials mailed?	Prohibition on requiring the transmission of unencrypted SSNs over the internet?	Other Prohibitions?	Exemptions?	Statutory Enforcement?	Statutes
Nevada	No	No	No	No	N/A	N/A	N/A	
New Hampshire	No	No	No	No	N/A	N/A	N/A	
New Jersey	Yes	Yes	Yes	Yes	Yes	Yes	No	N.J. Stat. Ann. §§ 56:8-164; 47:1-16
New Mexico	Yes	Yes	Yes	Yes	Yes	Yes	No	N.M. Stat. §§ 57-12B-3, 57-12B-4 *(Protections apply to consumers)*
New York	Yes	Yes	Yes	Yes	No	Yes	Yes	N.Y. Gen. Bus. Law § 399-DD

APPENDIX

	Prohibition on public display of SSNs?	Prohibition on printing SSNs on cards used to access products or services?	Prohibition on printing SSNs on materials mailed?	Prohibition on requiring the transmission of unencrypted SSNs over the internet?	Other Prohibitions?	Exemptions?	Statutory Enforcement?	Statutes
North Carolina	Yes	Yes	Yes	Yes	Yes	Yes	Yes	N.C. Gen. Stat. §§ 75-62; 132-1.10
North Dakota	No	No	No	No	N/A	N/A	N/A	
Ohio	No	No	No	No	N/A	N/A	N/A	
Oklahoma	Yes	Yes	Yes	Yes	No	Yes	No	Okla. Stat. tit. 40, § 173.1 *(Prohibitions apply to employers)*
Oregon	Yes	Yes	No	No	Yes	Yes	No	Or. Rev. Stat. §§ 646A.602, .620 *(Protections apply to consumers)*

	Prohibition on public display of SSNs?	Prohibition on printing SSNs on cards used to access products or services?	Prohibition on printing SSNs on materials mailed?	Prohibition on requiring the transmission of unencrypted SSNs over the internet?	Other Prohibitions?	Exemptions?	Statutory Enforcement?	Statutes
Pennsylvania	Yes	Yes	Yes	Yes	Yes	Yes	Yes	74 Pa. Stat. Ann. §§ 201 to 204
Rhode Island	Yes	Yes	Yes	Yes	Yes	Yes	Yes	R.I. Gen. Laws § 6-48-8
South Carolina	Yes	Yes	Yes	Yes	Yes	Yes	Yes	S.C. Code Ann. § 37-20-180, -200
South Dakota	Yes	No	No	Yes	No	No	No	S.D. Codified Laws § 1-27-44 *(Prohibitions apply to state agencies and its political subdivisions)*
Tennessee	Yes	Yes	Yes	Yes	No	Yes	Yes	Tenn. Code Ann. §§ 4-4-125, 47-18-2110

	Prohibition on public display of SSNs?	Prohibition on printing SSNs on cards used to access products or services?	Prohibition on printing SSNs on materials mailed?	Prohibition on requiring the transmission of unencrypted SSNs over the internet?	Other Prohibitions?	Exemptions?	Statutory Enforcement?	Statutes
Texas	Yes	Yes	Yes	Yes	Yes	Yes	Yes	Tex. Bus. & Com. Code Ann. § 501.001 to .102
Utah	Yes	No	No	No	Yes	No	Yes	Utah Code Ann. § 13-45-301 to -401
Vermont	Yes	Yes	Yes	Yes	Yes	Yes	Yes	Vt. Stat. Ann. tit. 9, § 2440
Virginia	Yes	Yes	Yes	Yes	Yes	Yes	Yes	Va. Code Ann. § 59.1-443.2 to -444
Washington	No	No	No	No	N/A	N/A	N/A	

	Prohibition on public display of SSNs?	Prohibition on printing SSNs on cards used to access products or services?	Prohibition on printing SSNs on materials mailed?	Prohibition on requiring the transmission of unencrypted SSNs over the internet?	Other Prohibitions?	Exemptions?	Statutory Enforcement?	Statutes
West Virginia	No	No	No	No	N/A	N/A	N/A	
Wisconsin	No	No	No	No	N/A	N/A	N/A	
Wyoming	No	No	No	No	N/A	N/A	N/A	

Courtesy of Foley & Lardner, LLP

ENDNOTES

1. (Although an individual's identity may only be valued at $10, the aggregate value of a large number of identities collected during the theft significantly improves the profitability of the crime.) *See* Margaret Harding, *Motives of many hackers darker these days, security experts say*, The Columbus Dispatch (Ohio), Aug. 14, 2006, at F04, *available at* 2006 WLNR 22961381.

2. Kim Ode, *Protecting identity among the tell-all generation; One in three victims of identity theft last year was a college student, Star Tribune (Minneapolis, MN), Aug. 15, 2007, at 1E, available at LEXIS.*

3. Gregory Childress, *Student identity theft more frequent; More disposable income makes them target for criminals*, The Herald-Sun (Durham, NC), Sept. 15, 2008, at C1, *available at* LEXIS.

4. Michele Melendez, *ID thieves target students. College Students 'prime target' for identity theft*, Mobile Register (Alabama), Feb. 4, 2007, at F06, *available at* LEXIS.

5. Gregory Childress, *Student identity theft more frequent; More disposable income makes them target for criminals*, The Herald-Sun (Durham, NC), Sept. 15, 2008, at C1, *available at* LEXIS.

6. See Privacy Rights Clearinghouse, "Chronology of Data Breaches: Security Breaches 2005-Present," available at **http://www.privacyrights.org/data-breach** (last visited September 15, 2010).

7. Id.

8. Verizon Business, *2010 Data Breach Investigations Report,* July 28, 2010 (available at **http://www.verizonbusiness.com/resources/reports/rp_2010-data-breach-report_en_xg.pdf**, last visited August 18, 2010).

9. GLB is also known by its official name – the *Financial Services Modernization Act of 1999*, (Pub. L. 106-102, 113 Stat. 1338, enacted November 12, 1999).

10. "Identity Theft Red Flags and Address Discrepancies Under the Fair and Accurate Credit Transactions Act of 2003," 72 Fed. Reg. 63718 (Nov. 9, 2007).

11. Pub. L. 104-191 (1996).

12. Open Security Foundation, DatalossDB, **http://datalossdb.org/ statistics** (last visited October 1, 2010).

13. Id.

14. Lynn Dolan, *College Door Ajar for Online Criminals*, L.A. Times, May 30, 2006, available at **http://articles.latimes.com/2006/may/30/ local/me-hacks30**; Gina Smith, *Computer Breach at USC, Error left 1,500 students' data open to public*, The State (S.C.), Sept. 7, 2007, at A1, *available at* 2007 WLNR 17457221.

15. Randy Ludlow and Holly Zachariah, *Hacked off Data thefts leave Ohio University scrambling, students and alumni steaming*, Columbus Dispatch (Ohio), June 19, 2006, at 01A, *available at* **http://www.techzone360.com/news/2006/06/19/1686625.htm**; Editorial: *Trust in Ohio University is eroding*, Columbus Dispatch (Ohio), May 16, 2006, at 13A, *available at* 2006 WLNR 17815704.

16. Michele Besso, *Computer breach exposes 1,000 UD students' info; Dept. of Public Safety server was hacked into on April 8*, The News Journal (Wilmington, Del.), May 25, 2006, at 1B, *available at* LEXIS.

17. Gary Gentile, *Hackers target universities*, Charleston Gazette: The Associated Press (W.Va), Dec. 18, 2006, *available at* 2006 WLNR 22136268.

18. Elizabeth Rosen, *Experts Say Universities Susceptible to Data Breaches*, The Cornell Daily Sun, July 7, 2009, *available at* **http://www.cornellsun.com/section/news/content/2009/07/07/ experts-say-universities-susceptible-data-breaches.**

19. Gina Smith, *Computer Breach at USC, Error left 1,500 students' data open to public*, The State (S.C.), Sept. 7, 2007, at A1, *available at* 2007 WLNR 17457221.

20. Open Security Foundation, DatalossDB, **http://datalossdb.org/ statistics** (last visited October 1, 2010).

21. Verizon Business, *2010 Data Breach Investigations Report,* July 28, 2010 (available at **http://www.verizonbusiness.com/resources/ reports/rp_2010-data-breach-report_en_xg.pdf**, last visited August 18, 2010).

22. Id.

23. Id.

24. While much of this guide focuses on electronic information, state and federal regulators have been assertive in pursuing security incidents over improperly discarded trash containing sensitive employee, consumer, and patient information. For examples, see the FTC's enforcement pages on the agency's website, While the retail pharmacy operations of CVS Caremark and Rite Aid have been prosecuted by the FTC and HHS for improperly discarding trash, a university hospital holds largely the same types of hardcopy and electronic information that these two companies allegedly lost.

25. Open Security Foundation, DatalossDB, Data Loss Statistics, **http://datalossdb.org/statistics?timeframe=last_month** (last visited October 1, 2010).

26. Id.

ENDNOTES

27. George Agathos, *Personal Information of up to 90,000 Compromised at Stony Brook*, Stony Brook Independent (N.Y.), May 19, 2007, *available at* **http://www.sbindependent.org/node/1850**; *Data Disclosure: Frequently Asked Questions;* Stony Brook University, *available at* **http://www.stonybrook.edu/sb/disclosure/**.

28. Id.

29. Id.

30. Open Letter from H. David Lambert, Vice President and Chief Information Officer to Tara Johnson, U.S. Department of Education (Feb. 29, 2008) (on file with Off. of Maryland Att'y Gen.), *available at* **http://www.oag.state.md.us/idtheft/Breach%20Notices/ITU-151124.pdf**.

31. Press Release: *Georgetown University Notifies Current and Former Students, Faculty and Staff of Data Breach*, **http://identity.georgetown.edu/45051.html** (last visited October 3, 2010).

32. Martin H. Bosworth, *Data Thieves Hit Georgetown University Students, Faculty*, ConsumerAffairs.com, January 30, 2008, *available at* **http://www.consumeraffairs.com/news04/2008/01/georgetown.html**.

33. Id.

34. University News: *Intensified Security Efforts Follow Data Breach*, *available at* **http://explore.georgetown.edu/news/?ID=31245** (last visited October 3, 2010).

35. *Security Breach Leaves 45,000 at Risk of Identity Theft*, The Cornell Daily Sun, June 24, 2009, *available at* **http://cornellsun.com/node/37474**.

36. Id.

37. Id.

38. Id.

39. Brian McNeill, *Thieves steal $22,000 using credit card of U.Va. professor; Data breaches at university had compromised his name and social security number*, Richmond Times Dispatch (Virginia), June 10, 2008, at B5, *available at* LEXIS.

40. Mel Beckman, *Your Laptop Data is Not Safe. So Fix It*, PC World Business Center, Jan. 20, 2009, *available at* http://www.pcworld.com/businesscenter/article/157966/your_laptop_data_is_not_safe_so_fix_it.html.

41. Elinor Mills, *Cloud computing security forecast: Clear skies*, CNET News Security, Jan. 27, 2009, *available at* http://news.cnet.com/8301-1009_3-10150569-83.html.

42. Mel Beckman, *Your Laptop Data is Not Safe. So Fix It*, PC World Business Center, Jan. 20, 2009, *available at* http://www.pcworld.com/businesscenter/article/157966/your_laptop_data_is_not_safe_so_fix_it.html.

43. *Biggest Insider Threat? Sys admin gone rogue*, http://www.networkworld.com/news/2010 citing the Verizon 2010 Data Breach Investigations Report (Sept. 28, 2010).

44. Open Security Foundation, DatalossDB, http://datalossdb.org/statistics (last visited October 1, 2010).

45. Michelle Hatfield, *UC Reveals Merced Data Theft: 1,300 Campus Employees Affected; Social Security Numbers Included*, Modesto Bee (Cal.), Dec. 13, 2006, at A, *available at* 2006 WLNR 21528871; Identity Theft: Innovative Solutions for an Evolving Problem: Hearing Before the S. Subcomm. on Terrorism, Technology, and Homeland Security of the Comm. on the Judiciary, 110th Cong. 3 (2007) (Testimony of Jim Davis, Associate Vice Chancellor, Information Technology).

46. Sean O'Sullivan, *Ex-Student guilty in hacking; Changing UD test date costs N.J. man $10,457, probation,* The News Journal, Apr. 26, 2006, at 1B, *available at* LEXIS.

47. Id.

48. Doug Hoagland, *Grand Jury Indicts 2 ex-CSUF students; Charges brought in computer hacking incident,* The Fresno Bee (Cal.), Nov. 1, 2007, at B1, *available at* LEXIS ; John Ellis, *No jail in grade changes at CSUF; Former Fresno State student gets probation in computer hacking scheme,* The Fresno Bee (Cal.), Aug. 16, 2008, at B1, *available at* LEXIS.

49. Id.

50. Randy Ludlow and Holly Zachariah, *Hacked off Data thefts leave Ohio University scrambling, students and alumni steaming,* Columbus Dispatch (Ohio), June 19, 2006, at 01A, *available at* LEXIS; Melissa Ezarik, *Ouch -- data theft,* University Business, August 1, 2006, at 15, *available at* 2006 WLNR 24446131.

51. Randy Ludlow, *Hackers again hit data at Ohio U.: Social Security info at least partially stolen,* Columbus Dispatch (Ohio), June 9, 2006, *available at* 2006 WLNR 9911791.

52. Carrie Ghose, *Attorneys seek to renew dismissed lawsuit over OU data breach,* Business First (Columbus, Ohio), Aug. 30, 2007, *available at* 2007 WLNR 16932573.

53. Randy Ludlow, *OU puts $8 million toward security computer system: Thousands still trying to steal data,* Columbus Dispatch (Ohio), July 29, 2006, *available at* 2006 WLNR 13125065.

54. Carrie Ghose, *Attorneys seek to renew dismissed lawsuit over OU data breach,* Business First (Columbus, Ohio), Aug. 30, 2007, *available at* 2007 WLNR 16932573.

55. *Two Grads Sue OU Over ID Theft Social Security Numbers Stolen*, Cincinnati Post (Ohio), July 27, 2009, at A2, *available at* 2006 WLNR 11186397.

56. Randy Ludlow, *OU faces suit over data loss: Alumni seek class-action status, call for university to pay credit monitor*, Columbus Dispatch (Ohio), June 27, 2006, *available at* 2006 WLNR 11129896.

57. Id.

58. Jim Phillips, *McDavis explains how, why computer system was breached*, Athens News (Ohio), Apr, 10, 2008, *available at* 2008 WLNR 7594403.

59. Id.

60. Editorial, *OU's identity theft caused by negligence*, Columbus Dispatch (Ohio), May 17, 2006, at 08A, *available at* 2006 WLNR 17816377.

61. Randy Ludlow and Holly Zachariah, *Hacked off Data thefts leave Ohio University scrambling, students and alumni steaming*, Columbus Dispatch (Ohio), June 19, 2006, at 01A, *available at* LEXIS; Editorial: *Trust in Ohio University is eroding*, Columbus Dispatch (Ohio), May 16, 2006, at 13A, *available at* 2006 WLNR 17815704.

62. Id.

63. Identity Theft Resource Center, Identity Theft: The Aftermath 2008, at 3 (June 30, 2009), *available at* **http://www.idtheftcenter. org/artman2/uploads/1/Aftermath_2008_20090520.pdf**.

64. Id.

65. Id.

66. Identity Theft Resource Center, Identity Theft: The Aftermath 2008, at 21 (June 30, 2009), *available at* **http://www.idtheftcenter. org/artman2/uploads/1/Aftermath_2008_20090520.pdf.**

67. Identity Theft Resource Center, Identity Theft: The Aftermath 2008, at 23 (June 30, 2009), *available at* **http://www.idtheftcenter. org/artman2/uploads/1/Aftermath_2008_20090520.pdf.**

68. Id.

69. Identity Theft Resource Center, Identity Theft: The Aftermath 2008, at 13 (June 30, 2009), *available at* **http://www.idtheftcenter. org/artman2/uploads/1/Aftermath_2008_20090520.pdf.**

70. Id.

71. "Fighting Back Against Identity Theft" available at **http://www.ftc. gov/bcp/edu/microsites/idtheft/consumers/about-identity-theft. html**

72. Id.

73. "Official Identity Theft Statistics," (Javelin Strategy and Research, 2009), available at **http://www.spendonlife.com/guide/ identity-theft-statistics**

74. In 2009, credit card fraud (17%) was the most common form of reported identity theft, followed by government documents/ benefits fraud (16%), phone or utilities fraud (15%), and employment fraud (13%). Other significant categories of identity theft reported by victims were bank fraud (10%) and loan fraud (4%). *See*, "Consumer Sentinel Network Data Book for January – December 2009," Federal Trade Commission, (February 2010), available at **http://www.ftc.gov/sentinel/reports/sentinel-annual-reports/sentinel-cy2009.pdf.**

75. "Fighting Back Against Identity Theft" available at **http://www.ftc. gov/bcp/edu/microsites/idtheft/consumers/about-identity-theft. html**

76. Id.

77. Federal Trade Commission – 2006 Identity Theft Survey Report, p.4

78. It has been estimated that 44% of consumers view their credit reports using AnnualCreditReport.com. One in seven consumers receive their credit report via a credit monitoring service. *See*, "Official Identity Theft Statistics," (Javelin Strategy and Research, 2009), available at **http://www.spendonlife.com/guide/identity-theft-statistics**

79. Identity theft "About Identity Theft" available at **http://www.ftc.gov/bcp/edu/microsites/idtheft/consumers/about-identity-theft.html**.

80. "Official Identity Theft Statistics," (Identity Theft Resource Center Aftermath Study, 2004), available at **http://www.spendonlife.com/guide/identity-theft-statistics**. It should be noted that the discovery period significantly differs depending on the type of fraud experienced. *See*, "Federal Trade Commission – 2006 Identity Theft Survey Report," prepared by Synovate (November, 2007), available at **http://www.ftc.gov/os/2007/11/SynovateFinalReportIDTheft2006.pdf**

81. "Official Identity Theft Statistics," (Identity Theft Resource Center Aftermath Study, 2004), available at **http://www.spendonlife.com/guide/identity-theft-statistics**

82. "Official Identity Theft Statistics," (Javelin Strategy and Research, 2009), available at **http://www.spendonlife.com/guide/identity-theft-statistics**

83. "Official Identity Theft Statistics," (Identity Theft Resource Center Aftermath Study, 2004), available at **http://www.spendonlife.com/guide/identity-theft-statistics**

ENDNOTES

84. "Federal Trade Commission – 2006 Identity Theft Survey Report," prepared by Synovate (November, 2007), available at **http://www.ftc.gov/os/2007/11/SynovateFinalReportIDTheft2006.pdf**

85. "Identity Theft Red Flags and Address Discrepancies Under the Fair and Accurate Credit Transactions Act of 2003," 72 Fed. Reg. 63718 (Nov. 9, 2007).

86. 15 U.S.C. § 1681 et seq.

87. 15 U.S.C. §§ 41-58.

88. GLB is also known by its official name – the *Financial Services Modernization Act of 1999*, Pub.L. 106-102, 113 Stat. 1338, enacted November 12, 1999.

89. 15 U.S.C. § 45(a)(1).

90. *General Offers and Claims Products and Services*, **http://www.ftc.gov/bcp/conline/pubs/buspubs/ruleroad.shtm**, last visited June 3, 2008.

91. *See, e.g., In the Matter of Rite Aid Corporation*, Agreement Containing Consent Order, July 27, 2010, available from **http://www.ftc.gov/os/caselist/0723121/100727riteaidagree.pdf**.

92. *In the Matter of the National Research Center for College and University Admissions, Inc., and American Student List, LLC, and Don M. Munce*, Complaint, January 28, 2003, available from **http://www.ftc.gov/os/2003/01/nrccuacmp1.htm**.

93. *In the Matter of Gateway Learning Corp.*, 2004 WL 2618647 (F.T.C. 2004).

94. 45 C.F.R. § 160.103.

95. *See, e.g., Community Hospital Group, Inc. v. Blume Goldfaden Berkowitz Donnelly Fried & Forte, P.C.* , 384 N.J. Super. 251 (App. Div. 2006); *University of Colorado Hosp. v. Denver Pub. Co.,* 340 F. Supp.2d 1142, 1144 (D. Colo. 2004); *Johnson v. Quander,* 370 F. Supp.2d 79 (D.D.C. 2005), *Poli v. Mountain Valleys Health Centers, Inc.,* 2006 WL 83378 (E.D. Cal 2006), *Silva v. Porter,* 18 A.D. Cas. (BNA) 483, 2006 WL 1890194 (M.D. Fla. 2006), and *Agee v. U.S.,* 72 Fed. Cl. 284, 289-290 (2006).

96. 18 U.S.C.A. §§ 2510-22; 2701-12.

97. 18 U.S.C.A. § 1030.

98. 18 U.S.C.A. § 2510-2511.

99. 18 U.S.C.A. § 1030.

100. *See, e.g., Trikas v. Universal Card Services Corp.,* 351 F.Supp.2d 37 (E.D. NY 2005), *Dyer v. Northwest Airlines Corporation,* 334 F. Supp.2d 1196, 1198 (D. N.D. 2004), *Stollenwerk v. Tri-West Healthcare Alliance,* 2005 WL 2465906 *1(D. Ariz. 2005) and *Bell v. Acxiom,* 2006 WL 2850042 (E.D. Ark. 2006).

101. *See* **http://www.pcisecuritystandards.org**.

102. Nev. S.B. No. 227.

103. RCW 19.255.020.

104. The Payment Card Industry Data Security Standards are generally available at www.pcisecuritystandards.org.

105. Privacy of Consumer Financial Information, 16 CFR Part 313.

106. Standards for Safeguarding Customer Information, 16 CFR Part 314.

107. GLB is also known by its official name – the *Financial Services Modernization Act of 1999*, (Pub.L. 106-102, 113 Stat. 1338, enacted November 12, 1999).

108. 65 Fed. Reg. at 33648.

109. Standards for Safeguarding Customer Information, Final Rule, summary, published in 67 Fed. Reg. 36484.

110. While regulators and courts will not typically require that an organization be on the leading edge of technology adoption to safeguard information, court decisions dating back nearly 80 years conclude that if mechanisms are reasonably available, then it will not matter that others (other schools, for example) have not adopted these technologies and practices. *See, e.g., In re Eastern Transportation Co. (The TJ Hooper)* 60 F.2d 737 (2d Cir.), cert. Denied, 287 U.S. 662 (1932).

111. 16 CFR 314.1(a).

112. 16 CFR 314.1(b).

113. 16 CFR 314.2(b)-(d).

114. 16 CFR 313(n)(1) (Privacy Rule definitions section).

115. 16 CFR 313(o).

116. 16 CFR 314.3(a).

117. 16 CFR 314.3(b).

118. **http://www.darkreading.com/story/showArticle.jhtml?articleID=225702686** last visited July 9, 2010.

119. 34 CFR Part 99.

120. 34 CFR 99.37(d).

121. 797 F.Supp. 1246 (D.N.J. 1992).

122. Columbia University policy: Social Security Number (SSN) and Unique Person Number (UPN) Usage, available at **http://www.columbia.edu/cu/administration/policylibrary/policies/cuit/00bb9 c6714dca2270114f656b5830003.html** (last visited December 22, 2010)

123. Id.

124. Id.

125. New York City Administrative Code 20-117. While this law has many features in common with the state breach notification laws, for the purposes of this chapter, municipal level laws are outside the scope. The chapter will specifically focus on the 46 state laws, as well as those in the District of Columbia, Puerto Rico and the U.S. Virgin Islands. Currently, Alabama, Kentucky, New Mexico, and South Dakota have no breach notification laws.

126. The law, California Civil Code §1798.82, became effective July 1, 2003.

127. California Civil Code §1798.82(h).

128. Wyoming Statutes §40-12-501(a)(vii)

129. District of Columbia *Consumer Personal Information Security Breach Notification Act of 2006*, §28-3851(1).

130. Haw. Rev. Stat. §487N-2(a).

131. New Hampshire *Right to Privacy Act*, §359-C:20(I).

132. North Carolina *Identity Theft Protection Act*, §75-65(a).

133. Wisc. Stat. §134.98(2)(a).

ENDNOTES

134. Del. Code §12B-102a.

135. Louisiana Database Security Breach Notification Law §3074(G).

136. New Jersey Permanent Statutes Title 56:8-163, §12(a).

137. While most of the laws that contain this exception to notification do not provide a set retention period, the New Jersey law requires that documentation of data breach investigations where notification is not provided be maintained for five years.

138. Florida Statutes §817.5681(1)(a).

139. Ohio Revised Code Ch. 1349.19, § B.

140. Wisconsin Statutes §134.98(3).

141. Recommended Practices on Notice of Security Breach Involving Personal Information. California Office of Privacy Protection. **http://www.privacy.ca.gov/res/docs/pdf/COPP_Breach_Reco_ Practices_6-09.pdf**. Last accessed March 20, 2010.

142. Massachusetts M.G.L. Chapter 93, §3(b) prohibits notification to affected individuals from including a description of the nature of the breach and the number of affected individuals.

143. *Id.*

144. The Wisconsin law does not preclude the use of e-mail as a form of notification where it has been used previously to communicate with individuals or its use is reasonably calculated to provide actual notice and the organization cannot ascertain through due diligence the mailing address of individuals. Wisconsin Statutes §134.98(3).

145. Pub. L. No. 106-229, 114 Stat. 464 (2000)(codified at 15 U.S.C. § 7001 *et seq.*)

146. In some jurisdictions, not only the state, but also affected individuals may enjoin organizations from failing to comply with the law.

147. Alaska *Personal Information Protection Act*, §45.48.080(a)(1).

148. Ohio Revised Code §1349.192 and Florida Statutes §817.5681(1) (b).

149. California Civil Code §1798.84(b).

150. Del. Code Ann. Tit. 6 §12B-104(a).

151. D.C. Code §28-3853(a).

152. Haw. Rev. Stat. §487N-3(b).

153. 815 ILSC 530/20 makes a violation of the law an unlawful practice under the *Consumer Fraud and Deceptive Business Practices Act*. Section 10a of the *Consumer Fraud and Deceptive Business Practices Act* allows any person who has suffered actual damages as a result of a violation of that Act.

154. La. Rev. Stat. Ann. §3075.

155. Md. Code Ann., Com. Law §14-3508 makes a violation of the law an unfair or deceptive trade practice. The enforcement and penalties provisions in Title 13 Consumer Protection Act, authorizes any person to bring an action to recover for injury or loss sustained by him as a result of a practice prohibited by that title (§13-408(a)).

156. N.H. Rev. Stat. Ann. §359-C:21(I).

157. N.C. Gen. Stat. Ann. §75-65(i).

158. Puerto Rico Law 111, Article 8.

159. S.C. Code Ann. §39-1-90(G)(1)-(4).

160. Tenn. Code Ann. §47-18-21(h).

161. Virgin Islands *Identity Theft Prevention Act* §2211.

162. Va. Code Ann. §18.2-186.6(A)(4)(I).

163. Wash. Rev. Code Ann. §19.255.010(10)(a).

164. 201 CMR 17.00.

165. NRS 597.970

166. Michigan Senate Bill 1022. **http://www.legislature.mi.gov/documents/2007-2008/billintroduced/Senate/pdf/2008-SIB-1022.pdf**

167. Washington Senate Bill 6425. **http://apps.leg.wa.gov/documents/billdocs/2007-08/Pdf/Bills/Senate%20Bills/6425.pdf**

168. NIST Special Publication 800-122 *Guide to Protecting Confidentiality of Personally Identifiable Information* at p. 3-2, available from **http://csrc.nist.gov/publications/nistpubs/800-122/sp800-122.pdf**.

169. Id. at p. 3-3 and 3-4.

170. Institutions with information on Massachusetts residents, for example, should be aware of the data security regulations that became effective on March 1, 2010. These are available at 201 CMR 17.00 and are quite specific as to what must go into an organization's comprehensive information security policy.

171. NIST Special Publication 800-122 at pp. 4-2 and 4-3.

172. *See, e.g., Telectron, Inc. v. Overhead Door Corp.*, 116 F.R.D. 107 (S.D. Fla. 1987).

173. *See, e.g., Applied Telematics, Inc. v. Sprint Communications Co.,* 1996 U.S. Dist. LEXIS 14053 (E.D. Pa. 1996).

174. *See, Lewy v. Remington Arms Co.,* 836 F.2d 1004 (8th Cir. 1988) (holding a company's document retention plan to a reasonableness standard).

175. NIST Special Publication 800-122 at pp B-4.

176. Michelle Hatfield, *UC Reveals Merced Data Theft: 1,300 Campus Employees Affected; Social Security Numbers Included,* Modesto Bee (Cal.), Dec. 13, 2006, at A, *available at* 2006 WLNR 21528871; Identity Theft: Innovative Solutions for an Evolving Problem: Hearing Before the S. Subcomm. on Terrorism, Technology, and Homeland Security of the Comm. on the Judiciary, 110th Cong. 3 (2007) (Testimony of Jim Davis, Associate Vice Chancellor, Information Technology).

177. Jaikumar Vijayan, *Breach at UCLA exposes data on 800,000: Intrusion was undetected for more than a year,* Computer World, Dec. 12, 2006, *available at* **http://www.computerworld.com/s/ article/9005925/Breach_at_UCLA_exposes_data_on_800_000_;** Identity Theft: Innovative Solutions for an Evolving Problem: Hearing Before the S. Subcomm. on Terrorism, Technology, and Homeland Security of the Comm. on the Judiciary, 110th Cong. 4 (2007) (Testimony of Jim Davis, Associate Vice Chancellor, Information Technology).

178. See Identity Theft: Innovative Solutions for an Evolving Problem: Hearing Before the S. Subcomm. on Terrorism, Technology, and Homeland Security of the Comm. on the Judiciary, 110th Cong. 3-4 (2007) (Testimony of Jim Davis, Associate Vice Chancellor, Information Technology).

179. See Identity Theft: Innovative Solutions for an Evolving Problem: Hearing Before the S. Subcomm. on Terrorism, Technology, and Homeland Security of the Comm. on the Judiciary, 110th Cong. 2 (2007) (Testimony of Jim Davis, Associate Vice Chancellor, Information Technology).

ENDNOTES

180. See Identity Theft: Innovative Solutions for an Evolving Problem: Hearing Before the S. Subcomm. on Terrorism, Technology, and Homeland Security of the Comm. on the Judiciary, 110th Cong. 4-5 (2007) (Testimony of Jim Davis, Associate Vice Chancellor, Information Technology).

181. See Identity Theft: Innovative Solutions for an Evolving Problem: Hearing Before the S. Subcomm. on Terrorism, Technology, and Homeland Security of the Comm. on the Judiciary, 110th Cong. 7 (2007) (Testimony of Jim Davis, Associate Vice Chancellor, Information Technology).

182. See Identity Theft: Innovative Solutions for an Evolving Problem: Hearing Before the S. Subcomm. on Terrorism, Technology, and Homeland Security of the Comm. on the Judiciary, 110th Cong. 8 (2007) (Testimony of Jim Davis, Associate Vice Chancellor, Information Technology).

183. See Identity Theft: Innovative Solutions for an Evolving Problem: Hearing Before the S. Subcomm. on Terrorism, Technology, and Homeland Security of the Comm. on the Judiciary, 110th Cong. 3 (2007) (Testimony of Jim Davis, Associate Vice Chancellor, Information Technology).

184. New York State Consumer Protection Board, *The New York State Consumer Protection Board's Privacy Guide: How to Handle Personal Identifiable Information and Limit the Prospects of Identity Theft*, October 2008.

185. Under the Massachusetts statute, the notification must <u>not</u> include the nature of the breach or unauthorized acquisition or use or the number of residents of Massachusetts affected by the breach.

186. Vermont Attorney General Security Breach Notification Guidance, Appendix 1.

187. Federal Trade Commission, *Information Compromise and the Risk of Identity Theft: Guidance for Your Business*, June 2004.

188. Id.

189. New York State Consumer Protection Board, *The New York State Consumer Protection Board's Privacy Guide: How to Handle Personal Identifiable Information and Limit the Prospects of Identity Theft*, October 2008.

190. Connecticut Attorney General's Office, *Press Release: Attorney General, DCP Announce Top 25 Companies with CT Residents Affected by Bank of New York Mellon Data Breach, Bank to Provide Free Credit Protection*, May 30, 2008, at **http://www.ct.gov/ag/cwp/view.asp?Q=416454&A=2795f.**

191. These insurance products are not available to residents of the State of New York due to the state's insurance laws.

192. Vermont Attorney General Security Breach Notification Guidance.

193. California Department of Consumer Affairs – Office of Privacy Protection, *Recommended Practices on Notice of Security Breach Involving Personal Information* at 11-12, Feb. 2007.

194. California Department of Consumer Affairs – Office of Privacy Protection, *Recommended Practices on Notice of Security Breach Involving Personal Information* at 13, Feb. 2007.

ENDNOTES